BROADWAY PLAY PUBLISHING, INC.

W9-BWM-637

10:00

HIGH ENERGY MUSICALS FROM THE OMAHA MAGIC THEATRE

Printed
in USA

249 WEST 29 STREET NEW YORK NY 10001 (212) 563-3820

AMERICAN KING'S ENGLISH FOR QUEENS

Book and Lyrics by Megan Terry
Music by Lynn Herrick

   The author wishes to thank the Nebraska Committee for
the Humanities, the National Endowment for the Arts, the
Nebraska Arts Council, the Ford Foundaton and the
Guggenheim Foundation whose support in part made the
creation and production of AMERICAN KING'S ENGLISH FOR
QUEENS possible. I would also like to thank my dear and
brilliant humanist friends for the generous sharing of their
life-long work, research, opinions, feelings, sensibilities and
good company during the many seminars we held together.
With their magnanimous and discerning help, I was able to
write the play; they are: Moira Ferguson, PhD., Sarah Hoagland, PhD., Sr. Mary McAuley Gillgannon, R.S.M., PhD.,
Evelyn McLellan, PhD., Julia Stanley, PhD., Jacqueline St.
John, PhD., and Mary Williamson, PhD. A very special thanks
to Project Director, Andrea Sherman. I also thank the entire
Omaha Magic Theatre Company, the charming, entertaining
actors/dancers/singers: Wes Bailey, Mechelle Keller, Elisa
Stacy, Jim LaFerla, Lynn Herrick, Donna Young; the gifted
designers, Diane Degan and Elisa Stacy; the fine, talented
composers, Lynn Herrick and Donna Young; and the creative,
innovative, resourceful Director and superb performer, Jo
Ann Schmidman, Artistic Director of the Omaha Magic Theater. And thanks, too, to the wonderful people of Nebraska
who made up our audiences, whose comments and discussions
with us, far into many nights, helped us to realize and finalize
the script so that we may now share it with others.

                                              —Megan Terry
                                              Omaha, Nebraska

March - April 1978

Directed and Choreographed by: Jo Ann Schmidman
Set Design: Diane Degan
Set and Costume Execution: Wes Bailey, Mechelle Keller
Prop Design: Elisa Stacy

ORIGINAL CAST

DANIEL CONNELL .... Wes Bailey
JULIA CONNELL .... Lynn Herrick
SUSU CONNELL .... Elisa Stacy
KATE CONNELL .... Mechelle Keller
DOUG CONNELL .... Jim LaFerla
JAIMIE CONNELL .... Donna Young
SILVER MORGAN CONNELL .... Jo Ann Schmidman
RABBIT .... Carmen Miranda

These Nebraska humanists provided original research and
the expertise of their disciplines to the Omaha Magic Theatre
via seminars, individual interviews, published articles, papers
and books in their fields in the conception, execution and
preparation of this musical play:

Moira Ferguson, PhD. − English
Sarah Hoagland, PhD. − Philosophy
Sr. Mary McAuley Gillgannon, RSM, PhD. − History
Evelyn McLellan, PhD. − English
Julia Stanley, PhD. − Linguistics
Jacqueline St. John, PhD. − History
Mary Williamson, PhD. − Communications

The Omaha Magic Theatre is a non-profit educational foundation.

This program was made possible in part by the Nebraska Committee for the Humanities (a state-based program of the National Endowment for the Humanities), the National Endowment for the Arts, the Nebraska Arts Council and the Ford Foundation.

CAST

SILVER MORGAN: A feral child, about 17 years
JULIA CONNELL: Mommie, 38, homemaker
DANIEL CONNELL: Dad, in his 40's, an Agribusiness executive
SUSU CONNELL: 16 years
KATE CONNELL: 11 years
DOUG CONNELL: 9 years
JAIMIE CONNELL: 6 years

At the Omaha Magic Theatre the children were played by adult actors. This will work for the actor and the audience if the actor works to project the child within. (Please don't play *at* being a child.) If adults do play the children, you might put the ages of the children in your program, if you think it will aid audience orientation.

It is also fine to have children play these roles.

THE SET

At the Omaha Magic Theatre we knew from the start that the piece we were developing with Megan Terry would be toured. We needed a light, packable set. The musical takes place in a middle-class American home.

Our Set Concept: A large doll house with removable panels. To achieve this, a frame was built using 3/4" inch plumber's pipe on which six 5' X 5' sewn soft-sculpture panels were hung: the Family Room (for this main-action area we used two panels—one of Dad's library and easy chair, the other of the kids's half of the room and the TV set), the Kitchen, the Bedroom, the Bathroom and Outdoors (the Prairie, home of the Snipe). Another panel needed in the second act was the Snipe Cage.

The Fabrics for the room panels must be carefully selected (flat textures and colors) so as not to upstage the actors performing in front of them. (*The Costumes*, on the other hand, may be of the brightest satins—exaggerated doll's clothes or beautifully made clothing of the 1950's. The family may look like a relay team, Olympic players—after all, a family must make it through the years together.) The *Snipe Bag* is made of bright tubular stretch material sewn at the bottom, draw string at the top and must be large enough to contain the woman playing Silver Morgan.

The actors make all scene and time changes.

How it Works: A room panel is brought forward to a 5 1/2' X 5' movable frame on wheels when the scene takes place in that room. This brings the scene change (the "where" transformation) into closer focus for the audience.

The Cranky: In the Omaha Magic Theatre production we constructed and used a Cranky, which we placed Downstage Right to inform the audience of the time that passes between scenes. The Cranky is a wooden or cardboard box with a large, square opening in the front and two dowels (cardboard rollers) running horizontally across top and bottom. Each dowel extends about 2" from each side of the box to make handles for rolling the paper. Time and scene changes are lettered boldly on a long roll of paper, with plenty of space between them. Top end of paper is glued to top dowel and rolled clockwise, bottom end glued to bottom dowel and rolled counter-clockwise.

Lights: Two hand-held lights, Downstage Right and Left, were used in the Omaha Magic Theatre production. They were used as "follow spots" for musical mumbers and to "bump up" stage lighting as "specials" when needed.

The above set, costume and lighting description is to serve the director and designer as suggestions—an example of just one of the many possible directions the set and costume conceptions could take.

ACT ONE

SCENE ONE

The lights are pre-set as audience enters. Room panels are in position. The audience views all rooms of the Connell home, front wall removed.

A Cranky, Downstage R., reads: "The Play Takes Place Over a Period of Several Days."

The family enters, DAD first, then DOUGIE, SUSU, MOM, KATIE and JAIMIE. DAD and MOM, in the pre-set light, remove the bedrooom panel from the second story of the house frame and place it on the movable frame, Center Stage. They unsnap the stretch coverlet and untuck the bottom of it. SUSU, KATE and JAIMIE (who have been engaged in pre-bedtime activities) pile in. While MOM and DAD kiss them and tuck them in, DOUGIE sneaks out, prodded by his sisters, and changes the Cranky to read "Thursday Night In Bed," then sneaks to piano unnoticed by MOM and DAD.

At the same time as the above action, SILVER MORGAN enters, totally covered inside the snipe bag, strutting like a "Miss America," to Downstage L., where she struggles and breaks out of bag. A spot illuminates her. She is costumed in brilliant colors as a rock or country-western star. Her long hair, once matted, is now in an incredible "do."

She welcomes the audience. She transforms the snipe bag throughout her speech into high-fashion accessories: A sash, a shawl, headgear, a sarong. Her speech and manner are like a "Miss America" after she's been five years on the road selling our "way of life."

SILVER: I'm happy to be with you here today. In the first part of our presentation we are going to introduce you to a family, a dear family who adopted me. Perhaps you've heard about human beings who've been raised by wolves, or bears. I had a similar experience. I was raised out here on the plains by prairie dogs. That's true. I don't know who my real parents are. I was found when just a tiny baby by a family of warm and affectionate prairie dogs. I was raised in their society. A great deal of my early life was spent underground, but we came out often to enjoy the sun, and to eat the delicious, nutritious and tough prairie grasses. I'm not sure of my exact age, but the dentist thinks I'm around the age of twenty, now. When found by my human family I may have been seventeen. I didn't know English. I spoke the language of my furry friends. (*Drops "Miss America" and her voice takes on the prairie dog sound. She makes two kissing sounds at audience and then begins* . . .) Bark, ark, chirk, birk, bark, mirk chirk chirk chirk. Brrrr. Brrrrrr. Kkk wuff wuff (*High howl*) arrrhhhhhh! Arrhhh! Woof wuff wuff irk. (*Miss America again*) The family Connell found me during the playing of a childhood game, which may be familiar to many of you. You will see it later on today (tonight). I adopted the language of my adopted family, English. But I still think in Prairie Dog and have to translate into your language. I like your language, and like to think about it and with it. A question that goes around and around in my mind is: "Do you bark like you think or think like you chirp? Do you bark, therefore, you are? Do you think like you talk, or talk like you think?" At the end of our presentation we'd like to have an open discussion where you may chirp and bark, whistle, or think, or even speak, if that is your inclination. I'm glad to see all of you. I really like to look at the hair on your heads . . .

In the first half of the show you'll get to know the Connells. But I want you to know these are events that happened in the family before I joined them. In the second half of the show, after a ten-minute intermission, you will see how this family helped me to make the transition from animal kind to mankind . . . womankind? Humankind? Our kind? English is such an expressive language, don't you (*Drops "Miss America" and her voice takes on prairie dog sound*) Ark? Bark? Chirk? Woof? Woof? Chirk? Bark bark? Mirk? Wuff wuff wuff ark ark bark chirk wuff bark bark?

SILVER MORGAN *drops her character and goes to get hand held light, which she focuses on* CHILDREN *in bed.* DOUGIE *at piano plays musical introduction to "You Speak English," While* DOUGIE *sings at piano the* GIRLS *sing entire song in bed, dancing under the covers.* MOM *and* DAD *right and left of bed attempt to settle their offspring.*

CHILDREN: Mama, O Mom-mom-mom-mom-mom-mee,

Ha ha ha ha ha ha, hee hee hee—Gee!
Gulch, mulch, ik mik kik, kik-kik-kee!
Mama? What do you call this—this Ahhhhh? This Eeeee?
Cat, dog, Daddy, Mommy. Bye-bye, Hi-hi-hi!
Shut up in the sky!
I—chocolate cake—hate you.
I love you, I do. I'm only fooling you!
I love to see you lose me in the grocery store.
I love you, I do. I'm only fooling you,
I hate you. Shut up!
    You fool! More roar!
    Watch me droo-oo-ool for you!
You, you. I'm hungry. When will I be big?
    What sound is this?
When I grow up, I'm gonna be a pig.
Big-gig-gig-gig-gig-gig-gig-gig Pig-gig-gig-gig-gig-gig-gig.
What sound is this, I said? I will not go to bed.
What is the name of the sound I make?
Tell me right now what sound is this?
This . . . (*Parents make kissing sound*) Kiss?
(*Parents make kissing sound*)
Tell me before I—Ahhhhhhhhhhhhhh!
Mom-mom-mom-mom-mom-mom-mom-mom-meeeee.
Ha, ha, ha. Hee hee hee, hee-Gee!
Mik-kik-kik-kik-kik, Muk-kuk-kuk-kuk-keee
Mama, what do you call this, this ahhhhhhh?

MOTHER: My darling, my beautiful baby dish—
Mama's honey, you're so funny.
You speak English, ah-ah-ah English, ah-ah-ah English, ah-ah-
ah-ah.

CHILDREN: Mee-mee-mee. I-I-I, I won't, I won't.
I want to, I want.
Wee-Wee-Wee
I want this.

MOM & DAD: (*Imitating kids*)
Wee-wee-wee!

CHILDREN: I want that.

MOM & DAD: Ke-ke-kee!

CHILDREN: I want zount . . .

MOM & DAD: Iglee!

CHILDREN: Count . . .

MOM & DAD: Biglee!

CHILDREN: (*Spoken*) English, why English?

JAIMIE: (*Spoken*) Why isn't it called Patricia?

KATE: Om-a-ha?

SUSU: Or Amerakish?

JAIMIE: I'm not speaking English,
I'm singing, I'm singing,
La-la-la-la-la-la
La-la-la-la-la-la-la,
La-la-la-la-la-la-la.

DAD: You're singing in English.

KATE: Grorr-rorr-rrunk-g-g-grunk.
No, I'm not, I'm singing pig!

CHILDREN: I'm big! I'm big! I'm singing pig!

SUSU: I speak star. Take me to your twinkle.

MOM: (*Crossing to* DAD) I speak clover. Roll over in your jar.

DAD: (*Crossing away from* MOM) I speak alfalfa.

JAIMIE: Oh, go blow! I speak crow.

KATE: I speak cow.

ALL: Moo-oo-oo-ooo!

KATE: (*Spoken*) I speak saucer.

JAIMIE: (*Spoken*) I speak Patricia.

SUSU: (*Spoken*)I speak Amerakish!

DAD: (*Spoken*)It's English! English!
(*Singing*) To speak all this you've had to use English.
All you know is your mother tongue.
And those words you learned from her
One by one.

DAD & MOM: (*Singing under kids*) Ah-ah, English, Ah-ah-ah, English . . .

CHILDREN: Why, why, why, why, why, why, why, why Do you say this? See? See? We want to name our own sound! See?

DAD: (*Sings to educate the audience as well as his own children*) I learned English from my mother. She learned English from *her* mother, Who learned English from her husband, Who *was* English. (*Spoken*) My grandmama was Spanish.

MOM: (*Spoken—crossing to* DAD) Who was Spanish?

DAD: (*Spoken*) My grandmama.

MOM: (*Spoken—crossing away from* DAD *to other side of bed*) You never told me that.

CHILDREN: (*Spoken*)We're Spanish! Ay ay! (*Sing—become Spanish dancers*) Caramba! Amigo! Arriba! Olé! Mu-cha-cha-cha-cha-cha-cha-cha-cha! Ay ay!

DAD: (*Simultaneously with kids—crossing to* MOM *for support in his lesson*) You're English. You speak English. My grandmama was Spanish, But she became English.

CHILDREN: (*Continuing*) Si Si mamacita, señor, señorita, Rosita, José, olé (O-LÉ!)

KATE: If she could change from Spanish to English, Then I can be a pig!

JAIMIE & SUSU: (*Ganging up on* KATE, *heads together*) You already are.

SUSU: (*Competing—better than her sisters*) You are, you are, but I'm a star!

KIDS, MOM *and* DAD *sing next three sections simultaneously.*

CHILDREN: Caramba, amigo, arriba, olé,
Muchacha-cha-cha-cha-cha-cha-cha,
Si si mamacita, señor, señorita,
Rosita, olé, English!

MOM: Mama's honey, you're so funny.
We speak English, so do you.
He speaks English, she speaks English,
I speak English.

DAD: I learned English from my mother.
She learned English from *her* mother,
Who learned it from her husband,
Who *was* English!

CHILDREN: Mom-mom-mom-mom-mom-mom-mom-mom-meeee!

SUSU: I'm a star!

KATE: I'm a pig!

JAIMIE: Ha ha ha,

SUSU: I'm a star, I'm a shining star!

JAIMIE: Hee hee hee hee, gee!

CHILDREN: If grandma could change from Spanish to English . . .

SUSU & KATE: Then I—can be a great big pig! Grunk grunk!

JAIMIE: Grunk grunk grunk, I'm a great big pig! Grunk grunk!

DAD: All you know is your mother tongue
And those words you learned from her one by one.
If you can learn English,
I can be a great big pig! Grunk grunk!

MOM: Oh my darling, my beautiful baby dish,
Mama's honey, you're so funny.
If you can speak Amerakish,
I can be a great big pig! Grunk! grunk!

On final "grunk grunk," each strikes a pig pose. MOM *and* DAD *together, kneel in front of bed. Family freezes.*

SILVER MORGAN *turns out spot and changes Cranky to read: "Friday Morning Before Work."*

SCENE TWO

JAIMIE *and* SILVER *remove bed panel, replace it on second story of house frame and place easy-chair section of family room on movable frame, placing kitchen panel on reverse side. During set change,* KATE *and* DOUGIE *transform into* DAD'S *easy chair recliner. Action begins immediately, before panel change is completed.*

DAD *sits in recliner and reads paper. His paper has two eyeholes so he can read and see everything that's going on.* SUSU *enters with big transistor radio glued to her ear, humming or singing loudly with it. She walks by* DAD, *bends to give him an automatic kiss and continues out.* DAD *stops her, speaking from behind newspaper.*

DAD: I thought it was your turn to take out the garbage this week.

SUSU: *(Still absorbed in radio)* Yeah, but . . .

*Chair suddenly reclines—*KATE *as the back and* DOUGIE *as the footrest go down.*

DAD: What?

SUSU: I was, Dad. I was . . .

Chair returns to upright.

DAD: You're name's on the list.

SUSU: Yeah, but . . .

Chair again reclines suddenly.

DAD:What?

SUSU: *(Removing radio from ear, coming back to earth)* Dad?

DAD: *(Holding paper in lap)* What did you say?

SUSU: Dad, I was just saying . . .

DAD: *(Stands)* What did you say?

SUSU: I said, "Dad, I was just . . . "

DAD: (*Moves closer to* SUSU) No, no—before that.

SUSU: What?

KATE *and* DOUG *become another version of same chair—they stand, legs apart, facing each other, hands crossed and connected to make seat for* DAD. DAD *throws paper in direction of chair.*

DAD: Before that.

SUSU: I don't remember.

DAD: You don't remember? (*Picks up paper and goes to sit*)

SUSU: (*Pause*) I don't.

DAD: (*Leaps up, legs wide, into a challenging crouch*) You better remember, because once you remember . . . (*he tosses this off lightly and returns to chair*) you are going to forget you ever said it.

SUSU: (*In pain, racking brain*) What did I say? What did I say?

DAD: You don't remember?

SUSU: (*Sinks to knees*) No.

DAD: (*Stands, blows coach's whistle around his neck*) Come here everyone.

KATE, DOUG *and* JAIMIE *chase each other in, playing and rough-housing,* KATE *and* DOUG *each carry two four-by-four-inch by one-and-a-half-foot pieces of wood,* JAIMIE *carries four.*

DAD: I want the whole family here. There's a lesson here.

SUSU: (*Sinks*) Dad, please . . .

DAD: (*Grabs one of the kids as they run by*) Where's your mother? (*calls out*) Julia! (*all go into kitchen with their wood piece—movable frame is turned around so kitchen faces out*) Come on everybody, into the kitchen.

SUSU: (*beginning to cry*) Oh Dad . . .

DAD: (*Takes* SUSU'S *hand, drags her Down Center*) Everyone here?

All including SUSU, *who have been sitting on floor—girls on one side,* DOUG *facing them as if around kitchen table—sit straight up,*

*hands braced on wood 4 X 4's—they become themselves "at attention,"
being punished in straight chairs.*

DAD: (*To audience, making an example of* SUSU) Repeat what you
just said.

SUSU: I can't.

DAD: Can't means won't.

SUSU: I didn't say anything bad.

DAD: (*Looking deep in her eyes*) It was worse than bad. (*Steps
back*) It was stupid. (*Continues to pull away from her, using this
as an example of taking away love if she doesn't improve*) I will not
have a stupid child in this family.

SUSU: (*Shows remorse*) I'm sorry. What was it?

DAD: It was "yeahbut."

SUSU: What?

DAD: You heard me. (*Says it fast*) "Yeahbut!"

SUSU: I still don't know.

DAD: You say it *all* the time, and it's going to stop.

SUSU: (*Screams*) What is it?

DAD: (*Jumps around her like a bunny and yells*) I'm a "yeahbut,"
"yeahbut," "yeahbut!"

MOTHER *comes running.*

MOM: (*Mind elsewhere*) What's going on here?

DAD: (*Crosses to* MOM, *reprimands her*) Where have you been?

MOM: Ironing.

DAD: Didn't you hear me call?

MOM: I was listening to my stories.

DAD: (*Turns away, throws up arms—to audience*) Soap operas!
No wonder the kid is stupid.

SUSU: I'm not. I'm . . . an A-plus student.

DAD: Do you admit you said "yeahbut"? (*Turns his back on kids*)

SUSU: I never heard that before. What is it?

KATE: (*Waving raised hand as in school*) It's a rabbit without any teeth. (*She,* DOUG *and* JAIMIE *all laugh*)

DAD: (*Glaring*) Who asked you?

KATE: No one.

DAD: Then keep silent . . . (*Makes "pop" noise by slapping his hand over his pursed open mouth—kids all bite their tongues*) . . . until you are asked to contribute.

KATE: Yes, Dad. (*Quickly returns to her tongue-biting*)

DAD: (*To* SUSU) You don't recognize your own speech. Let me say it slower for you. (*Transforming into deep-voiced Dad*) "I thought it was your turn to take out the garbage." (*Transforms into* SUSU, *skipping Stage L. and humming tune* SUSU *was singing*) "Yeah . . . but. Yeah . . . but." (*Kids giggle, he gives them a look. They stop and sit up even taller.* DAD *continues in his own voice*) There is no such word as "yeahbut."

SUSU: (*Devilish*) It's not as bad as "hell" . . . (*Kids giggle*) and damn . . . and . . .

MOM *puts her hand over* SUSU'S *mouth before she can complete her thought: "love."*

MOM: Hush, darling.

DAD: (*Stands and turns away from them*) It's worse.

MOM: (*Crosses to* DAD) Oh? In what way?

DAD: (*To audience*) First of all, there is no such word in English as "yeahbut," I don't want other people to think my children stupid and uneducated. The way one speaks shows one's intelligence. (*Gently, to* SUSU) I don't want you to be careless in speech at home or in public. (*His anger wells up—he grabs the front of her shirt and pulls her to her feet*) And in the second place, "yeahbut" is a stall for time while you think up a lie! (*Releases her*)

MOM *and others transform into monkeys.* JAIMIE *makes monkey sound as she monkey—runs to* MOM. *All hang on* MOM *like baby monkeys. They listen and look except at* DAD.

DAD: We will not raise a pack of monkeys. Julia, I hold you partially responsible for this sloppiness. You have one week to improve—the whole family! (*He transforms, Stage R., into a computer putting items out and pulling them in.* JAIMIE *mouths* DAD'S *exact words and lectures her stuffed rabbit*) I will not have children who cannot speak properly. It's cost me $150,000 (One hundred and fifty thousand dollars) to bring you into the world and get you this far in school and society. If you each go to college that's another $150,000 apiece before you have your degrees. Life is no joke. (*Makes big policy statement*) There is no time for carelessness. (*Folds over from waist up, lifts head and finger*) Good speech means clear thinking. (*Beats his chest like Tarzan*) Do you understand? (*Quietly pleading*) Answer me!

MOM *and* CHILDREN *stare, biting lips, too scared to speak.* DAD *exits.*

KATE: (*Looks around to see if* DAD'S *gone, whispers*) Yeah—but. (*All giggle but* SUSU)

ALL: (*Gather around* SUSU, *make a pact with eyes*) Yeah—but!

*They giggle as they exit—*MOM *walking, kids hopping—rhythmically chanting "yeahbut." All freeze.*

SILVER MORGAN *changes Cranky to read: "Early Friday Afternoon."*

SCENE THREE

JAIMIE *sits down Center in front of big picture window facing out toward audience. She tries not to suck her thumb and sings a few bars of "Meow meow meow meow" the Purina cat food commercial. She sees something out window, hides from it and whispers to her stuffed rabbit. Both* JAIMIE *and* RABBIT *look out window.*

Meanwhile, DAD *and* DOUG *turn movable frame around so living room panel again faces out.*

MOM *dusts with oversize stuffed feather duster, dancing as she dusts, doing leaps and pirouettes and humming "You Speak English."*

JAIMIE: (*Looking out window*) The rabbit's eating our lettuce.

MOM: Is he?

JAIMIE: No. I said *the rabbit.*

MOM: He's eating the lettuce.

JAIMIE: No. *He* isn't eating the lettuce.

MOM: (*Drops duster, crosses to* JAIMIE *and hugs her*) *Who's* eating the lettuce?

JAIMIE: Yeah.

MOM: (*Tickles* JAIMIE'S *nose*) *He's* eating it.

JAIMIE: No. *He's* not.

MOM: I thought you said . . . (*Makes rabbit ears with her hands and buck teeth, munches*) "The rabbit is eating the lettuce."

JAIMIE: Yeah. (*Giggles*)

MOM: (*Tickles* JAIMIE) Why did you say no?

JAIMIE: Because *he's* not eating it—the rabbit is.

MOM: (*Returns to dusting*) That's what I said. He's eating the lettuce.

JAIMIE: (*Throws herself on floor*) No he isn't. *Daddy's* at work. Didn't you hear what I said?

MOM: Yes, darling, I did. You said he's eating the lettuce.

JAIMIE: (*Falls on stomach*) He can't eat the lettuce. He's at work. (*Runs to window*) The rabbit's eating the lettuce!

MOM: (*Gently reminding*) Don't shout at me.

JAIMIE: (*Crawls up and hugs* MOM) It's the rabbit. It isn't *he.* (*They hug*)

MOM: The rabbit. He's eating the lettuce.

JAIMIE: (*Jumps into* MOM'S *arms*) How do you know?

MOM: You told me.

JAIMIE: I did not. (MOM *drops her*)

MOM: (*Starts to slap her with feather duster but stops herself*) Stop that.

JAIMIE: I hate you.

MOM: (*Slaps her with bare hand*) Don't talk to me that way.

JAIMIE: You're stupid, stupid, stupid!

MOM: (*Takes hold of* JAIMIE) What's wrong with you?

JAIMIE: (*Matter of fact*) You're stupid.

MOM: (*Turns her around, face to face*) Look, we both agree the rabbit's eating the lettuce.

JAIMIE: (*Hugs* MOM *in relief that she understands*) The rabbit's eating the lettuce.

MOM: (*Firmly*) I said yes, he's eating the lettuce.

JAIMIE: (*Crawls away*) You're crazy.

MOM: You don't talk to me that way.

JAIMIE: (*Confronting* MOM) You told me Momma rabbits have babies.

MOM: Yes.

JAIMIE: How can *he* have babies?

MOM: He doesn't have babies, but he can eat lettuce.

JAIMIE: How do you know?

MOM: You told me.

JAIMIE: (*Runs away in utter frustration*) I did not tell you.

MOM: (*Confused*) You did.

JAIMIE: (*Jumps on each word*) I told you the rabbit is eating the lettuce.

MOM: Yes, he is.

JAIMIE: (*Angry*) He's not here. (*Mimes fixing tie, getting in car and driving to work*) He got in his car and went to his work. (*Looks out window, then flops down with back to window*) Anyway, the lettuce is all gone by now.

MOM: (*Shakes* JAIMIE) Why didn't you tell me sooner? (*Looks after her, trying to spank her but never coming close*) How can he have babies? How do you know he's eating the lettuce? *I* know he isn't eating lettuce. He's at work.

MOM: (*Gives up and goes back to dusting*) He's going to warm your bottom when he comes home.

JAIMIE: (*Sits down, mad*) You're crazy.

MOM: He's going to spank you when he comes home.

JAIMIE: No he won't. *He . . .* (*Sneaks up, pokes head between* MOM'S *legs*) won't be able to lift his arm, because he'll be too full of lettuce. You make me crazy, you stupid, stupid!

MOM: You go to your room.

MOM *goes back to dusting, dancing slower and humming a dirge.* JAIMIE *starts to leave, then is stopped by a message from her rabbit, whom she holds to her ear for the secret. Pleased with herself, she crosses to* MOM.

JAIMIE; If all the rabbits are boys, are all the cats girls?

MOM: (*Points to* JAIMIE'S *room*) March!

Three beats, then freeze!

SCENE FOUR

SILVER MORGAN *turns cranky to read: "Friday Afternoon Before Dad Comes Home."* KATE *and* DOUGIE *turn movable frame so kitchen panel faces front. There is a conspiracy in the making.* KATE *sends* SUSU *off to pretend to be kitchen table, center stage.* DOUGIE *hides under the table.* JAIMIE *is sent to the piano, and* KATE *transforms into a stew-pot, removing the stew from its hook on the kitchen panel and holding it as* MOM *stirs.* MOM *is self-involved, stirring the stew and sighing enormous sighs. She doesn't notice that* KATE *has replaced the pot. The stew is a large net with soft-sculpture vegetables attached to it. During "inner turmoil" chorus, the* CHILDREN *come out of their hiding places and transform into the stew that snares* MOM *in the net of domesticity.*

MOM: (*Sighs, then sings*) Where was I? Oh—
"Julie. Julie."
Who are you? Who are you?"

I'm Mrs. Daniel Connell,
And I'm making veal stew.

"Hello Julie. Hello Julie"

Was that my voice?
No choice.
There's nobody here.
(Spoken) It *was* my voice.

CHORUS: *(Children)* Oh the inner turmoil!
Oh the mental strife!
I'm driven crazy by this question:
What is the meaning of life?

MOM: "Hello Julie."

Shut up, I'm chopping parsley!
That voice is sixteen.
I haven't heard it
Since I walked through our soybeans,
Singing to the moon, singing to the moon,
All alone, Julie and my moon.

I've traveled thirty-eight times around the sun.

"Julie, you're sixteen. Life has just begun."

How can this be?
What's got into me?
"Julie, Julie. Let's have fun! Let's have fun!"

Shoo! Shoo! Shoo! *(Shoos away veal stew, net and* CHILDREN*)*
Got to make this veal stew!

CHILDREN *repeat chorus as the stew envelops* MOM. *She chops wildly at vegetables and struggles to escape.*

The CHILDREN *lead* MOM, *still in the stew net, upstage right where she stays. They transform back into themselves.* KATE *signals to* JAIMIE *and* DOUGIE *to follow her into family room by circling performance space. They turn frame around so family room faces front.* MOM *sighs from under the net, upstage R, four or five times during the following family-room scene.*

KATE *takes* JAIMIE *and* DOUGIE *by the hand, sits them on the floor, motions them to be quiet.*

KATE: What's wrong with Mom?

DOUGIE: Is something wrong?

KATE: She's been sighing a lot.

JAIMIE: What does that mean?

KATE: Like this. *(Sighs like* MOM*)*

DOUGIE: I've done that.

JAIMIE: When?

DOUGIE: When I can't do my homework.

JAIMIE: When I can't find my shoes.

DOUGIE: When you won't give me the electronic football game.

JAIMIE *mocks* DOUGIE.

KATE: Sighs are just the first steps before . . . *(Explodes—keeps it up during next three lines)*

JAIMIE: Not Mom.

KATE: You don't have a memory. *(Keeps exploding)*

DOUGIE: When did Mom explode?

KATE: When *her* mother calls her up and tells her to wear her rubbers, two sweaters, her fur coat and fur hat when it's snowing.

DOUGIE: Mom wouldn't blow up over that.

KATE: *(Digs heels in)* She hates to be told what to do.

KATE: She tells *us.*

KATE: She hates it, because she's grown up.

JAIMIE: Do you hate it?

KATE: I don't think so.

DOUGIE: Why should she?

Before each of the next three lines, the speaker does an "emblem" of how (s)he solves a problem. In O.M.T. production, KATE *writhes and mumbles,* DOUGIE *rocks, and* JAIMIE *shakes her thumb to keep from sucking it.*

KATE: Maybe she's worried.

JAIMIE: Maybe she's tired.

DOUGIE: Maybe she wants to run away from home.

Emblems stop.

KATE: She did it once.

JAIMIE: No she didn't.

KATE & DOUGIE: Yes she did.

JAIMIE: When?

DOUGIE: You're too little to remember.

KATE: I bet you don't remember either.

DOUGIE: She ran away to the Ramada Inn!

KATE: Nope, you dope, it was Howard Johnson's.

DOUGIE: How gross. *(Does his emblem)*

KATE: That's all the gas she had.

JAIMIE: *(Tugging at* DOUGIE'S *sleeve)* Why'd she run away to the Howard Johnson's.

DOUGIE: She was mad at Dad.

KATE: She was mad at all of us.

DOUGIE: Not at us?

KATE: Yes she was. She was mad at Dad and she was mad at you.

DOUGIE: Not me. I was too little.

KATE: You were a pain in the neck. You'd throw yourself on the floor and cry and stop breathing until you turned blue. Dad had to throw you in the air to get you breathing again.

DOUGIE: I don't believe it.

KATE: Yeah, you did it. Like this. *(Shrieks and holds breath.* JAIMIE *copies her to mock* DOUGIE.)*

DOUGIE: *(To* KATE*)* I did not! *(To* JAIMIE*)* I did not! You're mean.

GIRLS *still hold their breath.*

KATE: Shut up.

DOUGIE: Don't tell me to "shut up." You're not supposed to say that.

KATE: You said it.

DOUGIE: When?

KATE: You just said it.

DOUGIE: Yeah, but . . .

KATE: *(Hits him and releases breath)* You're not supposed to say that either.

DOUGIE: Mom!

KATE: *(Puts her hand over* DOUGIE's *mouth)* Shut up, dummy.

JAIMIE: *(Whisper)* Be quiet. Mom doesn't feel good.

DOUGIE: *(Sits down, rocks)* I'm going to tell.

KATE: That won't make her feel better, will it? Will it?

DOUGIE: I don't know. I don't know. I don't know.

KATE: Are you kidding? If you go in there screaming and crying, she's going to sigh more.

DOUGIE: You make *me* sigh. I bet you're the one who makes Mom sigh.

KATE: Try to think positive like Dad says to do.

JAIMIE: How can we cheer up Mom?

KATE: We could clean our room.

DOUGIE: *(Rocks)* Gross.

JAIMIE: *(Excited)* We could straighten up the family room.

DOUGIE: *(Crosses to* JAIMIE *and slaps at her)* You do that since you messed it up.

JAIMIE: I did not.

KATE: *(Takes their hands)* O.K., we'll clean it up, and then we'll blindfold her and bring her in to see it.

JAIMIE: That'll be fun.

KATE: *(Checks watch and crosses L to get game)* It's about forty-five minutes before Dad gets home.

JAIMIE: He likes us to be dressed up.

DOUGIE: We should get all clean and changed before we clean up here.

KATE: *(Sets soft sculpture game in center of floor—kids sit around it)* Let's finish this game first.

JAIMIE: *(Hugs KATE)* How much time is forty-five minutes?

DOUGIE: Oh, that's a long, long time. JAIMIE *crosses to* DOUGIE *and hugs him)*

JAIMIE: How long?

KATE: We could play this game two whole times through and still have time to get cleaned up and help Mom and set the table.

JAIMIE: Are you sure?

KATE: Of course I'm sure.

DOUGIE: *(Stands)* You're not always right, you know.

KATE: I've been right more often than I've been wrong.

JAIMIE: *(Innocently, through giggles)* You were really wrong about where women get babies.

KATE: *(Covers JAIMIE's ears)* What? You don't know about that!

JAIMIE: You said women got babies from wearing maternity clothes. *(Falls over on floor laughing)*

KATE: Get over here and play! Do you want to finish this game or not?

JAIMIE: O.K. O.K. O.K.

DOUGIE: *(Sits, turns away from others)* You're not always right, you know.

KATE: I admit it, O.K.? Play or get lost.

JAIMIE: *(Plays)* O.K. I'm playing.

KATE: Boys can be teachers. *(Dreams)* My teacher's a boy.

DOUGIE: That's our swimming teacher.

JAIMIE: *(Dreamy, in love)* Yep. He lets me ride on his back in the pool sometimes.

KATE: Boys can be principals. Our principal's a boy.

DOUGIE: *(Stands up and flies like a saint from his "Children's Bible" ilustration)* I'm a flier.

JAIMIE: Girls can be fliers. *(Mimics him)*

DOUGIE: *(Still flying)* Not in this game.

KATE: Stewardesses are fliers.

DOUGIE: *(Drops it)* They are not!

KATE: They are too!

JAIMIE: *(Crosses with tray of imagined food)* They go up in the plane and bring you things to eat. *(Stuffs it in DOUGIE's face)*

DOUGIE: They're waitresses. Just like at Pizza Hut.

KATE: They are not waitresses!

DOUGIE: *(Turning on her)* What's the difference? They wait on you when you're up in an airplane. *(Flying)* They don't drive the plane, you dope.

JAIMIE: *(Driving plane)* I'd drive the plane if something happened to the pilot. *(Points over her shoulder at DOUGIE)*

DOUGIE: You wouldn't know how.

KATE: What do you want to be when you grow up, Doug?

DOUGIE: *(Flying saint image)* I'm working on it all the time.

KATE: *(Sarcastically)* Flying?

DOUGIE: Some.

JAIMIE: *(Tugging on his sleeve)* What are you gonna be?

DOUGIE: I already am what I am. I just want to do more of it.

JAIMIE: Tell me?

DOUGIE: No. It's for me to know and you to find out.

JAIMIE: *(Hugs him)* Play with us, Dougie?

DOUGIE: *(Shakes loose—both sit)* What'll you give me?

JAIMIE: I'll give you my dessert.

DOUGIE: You hate dessert.

JAIMIE: That's true. I'd rather eat pickles.

KATE: *(Tickles him)* You're a pickle, Doug. It won't hurt you to play.

DOUGIE: *(Picks up card, runs off reading aloud)* "What Shall I Be? The Exciting Game of Career Girls." *(Tosses card on board)* I'd rather play "Sing Along with Cher." Go get the toy microphone.

KATE: That would mess up the place more. Let's finish this or nothing.

JAIMIE: *(Luring)* I'll give you one of my Indian Head cents that Grandma gave me.

DOUGIE: *(Thinks a second)* It's a deal! *(They shake hands)*

KATE: Are you sure you want to do that, Jaimie?

JAIMIE: Yep.

DOUGIE: If I get the ballerina cards I'm quitting.

KATE: A deal's a deal.

DOUGIE: I won't dance.

JAIMIE: You're a good dancer, Dougie.

DOUGIE: How do you know?

JAIMIE: *(Snaps fingers and rocks, mimicking DOUGIE)* I seen you in the tree house, dancing to your portable radio.

DOUGIE: *(Blushes, regains composure, says in toughest voice)* It wasn't dancing.

JAIMIE: Sure looked like it to me.

KATE: Men can be great dancers. That ballet dancer in that movie got a nomination for the Academy Award.

DOUGIE: He's so short.

KATE: *(Hitting him on head)* So are you. (GIRLS *giggle)*

DOUGIE: *(Stands)* I'm growing every day.

JAIMIE: *(Shakes dice)* Is it my turn?

DOUGIE: You're so little you can't even roll dice. *(Grabs at dice. He and* JAIMIE *roughhouse.)*

JAIMIE: You got a big mouth. *(Opens mouth wide)*

KATE: *(Calms them)* Shut up both of you and let's play.

DOUGIE: *(Leaps)* O.K. I'll be a ballet dancer if I have to . . . *(Sits)* but I'm never going to be a princess.

JAIMIE: *(Laughs)* That's not a princess, you dope.

DOUGIE: Who you calling a dope, dopey?

JAIMIEd: *(Cross to* DOUGIE *and hugs him)* I'm sorry I called you Dopey. *(Kisses him)* Your real name's Grumpy. *(Tickles him and runs away)*

DOUGIE: Your name's Tag-Along Tooloo, you little spy. *(Starts after her)*

KATE: *(Grabs* DOUGIE, *twirls him around till he's in his place)* That's not a princess, Doug, that's an actress. *(Rolls the dice)* O.K. I get a "Personality" card.

JAIMIE: Read it to me.

KATE: "You have patience." That's "good for being a ballet dancer, nurse or teacher."

JAIMIE: *(Rolling dice)* Give me my heart card. *(Tries to read it, holds it out to* KATE) Read it to me.

KATE: *(Reading)* "You are a quick thinker."

JAIMIE: Yes, I am.

KATE: That's "good for being an airline hostess and nurse."

JAIMIE: I like to make people well.

DOUGIE: You make me sick. (JAIMIE *makes a face at him.)*

KATE: Your turn to roll, Dougie.

DOUGIE: *(Prepares himself as he's seen it done in gangster movies: Squats, shakes dice, rolls)* Down and dirty.

JAIMIE: *(Jumps up, runs downstage shaking finger at* DOUGIE*)* Ummmmmm, Doug.

DOUGIE: *(Chases her)* I didn't say anything, you little pill!

KATE: Read your card, Doug.

DOUGIE: *(Reads it to himself)* No.

KATE: Read it out. We did.

DOUGIE: O.K. I'm glad! *(Reads)* "Your makeup is too sloppy. Bad for being airline hostess and model." *(Girls giggle hysterically)*

KATE: *(Dreaming)* I'd like to be a model.

DOUGIE: You're too fat.

KATE: *(Looks at self in imagined mirror)* I'm just right for my age. The school nurse said so.

DOUGIE: Look at the magazines. *(Pokes her)* You're too fat.

KATE: *(Pulls away)* What do you know about it?

DOUGIE: *(Stoops and lifts two very heavy objects in his hands, approaches* KATE*'s chest with them)* Them dames got no tits. you're already starting to push out your sweater.

JAIMIE: *(Shakes finger, threatening to tell)* Mom! Mom!

DOUGIE: *(Grabs* JAIMIE*'s arm and drags her around)* Shut up, you little spy. You wanted to play this game. You play it or I'll twist your arm off and shove it down your throat. *(*JAIMIE *runs to* KATE *for protection.)*

KATE: *(Straightening game)* Can't you even play a simple game?

DOUGIE: I didn't want to play. It's a stupid girl's game.

JAIMIE: *(Snatches up card and reads it out)* Here's Doug's card. *(She tries, but she's too little to read the big word)* "You are e-e-em-emo- . . . (*KATE *reads over her shoulder and whispers to her)* emotional. Good for model and actress."

DOUGIE: *(Screams and flails)* I am not emotional! I am not emotional!

KATE & JAIMIE: *(Fall in each other's arms laughing, chant mockingly at him)* You are pretty. You are graceful. You have a nice smile. You have correct posture, but you makeup's too sloppy. Too sloppy.

DOUGIE: *(Chants back)* Girls are crazy! Girls are crazy! Lazy-crazy!

MOM *sighs, interrupting* DOUGIE'S *line. When* KATE *hears this, she covers* DOUGIE'S *mouth.* JAIMIE *and* KATE *turn movable frame back to kitchen panel. All three hold net across width of stage in front of* MOM—*she's still trapped.*

MOM: *(Still chopping, sings)* Somewhere in this murk of me
There really may still lurk a me
Who's free.

KIDS *drape net over* MOM'S *head and hold ends like ladies-in-waiting.*

MOM: What is she like?
And where did she go
For the last twenty years or so?

KATE & DOUGIE *spin* MOM *in net, beat her with vegetables.*

CHORUS (CHILDREN): Oh the inner turmoil!
Oh the mental strife!
I'm driven crazy by this question:
What is the meaning of life?

MOM *sigh,* KATE *stuff carrot in her mouth,* DOUGIE *torments her with celery. They freeze, then move to next scene.*

SCENE FIVE

SILVER MORGAN *changes cranky to read "Saturday Before Dinner."*

JAIMIE *transform into kitchen table.* KATE *and* DOUGIE, *R and L on table, become kitchen chairs. They sit, knees up, holding their ankles.* MOM *sits on* DOUGIE'S *knees and chops a carrot on the table.* DAD *has moved the kitchen panel stage R, where he stirs the stew, swirling the net hooked on the kitchen panel.*

SUSU *comes in from a school activity.*

SUSU: *(Crosses to* DAD*)* Oh Dad! *(Crosses to* MOM *and kneels by her)* Oh Mom, I'm in love!

MOM: Who's the lucky guy?

SUSU: *(Starry-eyed)* Hank Dallas.

MOM: *(Chopping carrot)* He's cute.

SUSU: He's a dream. I'm in love. Was it like this for you, Mom?

DAD: I'm not fooling. Romantic love is neurotic. *(Sits)* Stop it right now.

SUSU: But it's nothing you can stop. *(Honestly)* I couldn't help it.

DAD: *(Picks up paper)* If you couldn't help it, then something has to be wrong with it.

SUSU: Mom, Mom, you don't feel that way, do you?

MOM: Wait a minute . . .

DAD: You're forbidden to see Hank Dallas again.

MOM: She's in his class in school—how can she help it?

SUSU *crosses center between* MOM *and* DAD *so only* MOM *can see her left arm.*

DAD: She can ignore him. *(Holds paper in front of face)*

SUSU: *(Secretly shows* MOM *a bruise on her arm)* Look here, Mom. Hank gave me a love punch.

DAD: *(Stands)* I heard that. And that proves it's sick. *(Kisses her forehead)* No more romance. It's nothing but grief.

MOM: *(Stands—slow cross downstage)* What do you mean? We haven't done so bad. (DOUGIE, *as chair, follows her downstage)*

DAD: *(Crosses down R)* We grew to love each other.

MOM: *(Striken—collapses in chair)* You mean you didn't love me when we were married?

DAD: I loved you as I loved all God's creatures.

MOM: *(Stands)* I was in love with you. Were you in love with me?

DAD: *(Crosses to stir soup)* It worked out because I was prudent. Your family and mine had good stock. Our children are healthy, marriage partnership sound. Why our net worth is two hundred thousand, counting our house and stock options. We've had no catastrophic illnesses. *(Goes to* SUSU, *who leaps up to attention)* Come here, child. I don't want you reading any more TV magazines or listening to Top 40 music.

MOM: *(Cross to* DAD—SUSU *is sandwiched in between)* What is this? You sound like Women's Liberation.

DAD: I beg your pardon.

MOM: What you just said is the party line of the radical feminists.

DAD: *(Nudges* MOM*)* If they agree with me, they must have sense. The feminist movement is nothing but a good old-fashioned puritan revolt against permissive new sex arrangements. *(Sits on* KATE *as chair)*

MOM: *(Pulls* SUSU *to her)* Come here darling. Your father likes to be like *his* father. He wasn't like this when he was young.

SUSU: *(Hugs* MOM*)* I'm in love with Hank Dallas. I can't help it. I don't want to help it.

DAD: *(Pulls* SUSU *downstage R)* Go to your room and do your math. *(Pushes her to room but keeps hold of her hand—she's pulled back)* You young people don't know the value of a dollar. *(Sends her off, pulls her back)* I'll help pick out your husband for you when the time comes. And it won't be that reckless Hank Dallas. *(Sends her off)*

SUSU: *(Starts to exit, stops herself before she's out, turns and stands up to* DAD*)* Then I'll never marry. This is America and I can do what I want, and work where I want, and love who I want, and you can't stop me.

DAD *lunges for her, she runs, they chase around table.*

DAD: *(During the chase)* As long as I buy your food, and provide shelter, you will do as I desire.

MOM: *(Crosses center, between them, and stops chase)* And what about what *I* desire?

DAD: *(A hug to calm* MOM*)* We both desire the best for our children. *(To audience)* I admire the Indian system. East Indian. All the marriages there are arranged, and only one in ten fail. That's more than you can say for our country. One out of every two marriages end in divorce.

SUSU: I hate statistics and I hate you. I'm going to run away to Alaska with Hank on his snowmobile. *(Starts to exit)*

DAD: Here, read the *Wall Street Journal.* You'll thank your old Dad one day.

He smacks SUSU *on bottom with newspaper. She turns front, shreds the* Wall Street Journal *and exits.*

MOM: *(Crosses to* DAD*, makes up to him)* Dan, please don't interfere with her right to dream and plan. You'll stifle her imagination.

DAD: *(Kneels, pressing face to* MOM*'s bosom)* All around us we see families falling apart. Children are raised not knowing the value of a dollar. *(Face to face with* MOM*)* You and I had to work for everything we've got. I think we should put the kids on salaries now. They're big enough to find out how the world works. *(To audience)* I'm sorry my parents weren't stricter with me. I'm forty-five, and it's only now that I see how the world works. I'm afraid it's too late to make it work for me, I mean us.

MOM: *(Strokes him)* Why are you so nervous?

DAD: I'm not nervous.

MOM: Then why did you attack our innocent child?

DAD: Because she's foolish. I will not have a foolish, dreamy child.

MOM: *(Floats dreamily downstage R)* But it's so beautiful.

DAD: *(Ducks bullets, hides in trenches, evading enemy fire)* The whole world is nipping at our heels. The Japanese and the Germans have sounder money than we do. The dollar is now worth four cents. (MOM *stands before firing squad)* The family system is eroding, and you want all our children to be dreamy and foolish. *(Flattens to ground, hiding)* That's how the rest of the world wants our children to be too. *(Brushes self off, gathers power and stands)* In ten years we'll all be such marshmallows, any tinhorn dictator can walk in and take us over.

MOM: This isn't like you, Dan. You sound like my old Uncle George.

DAD: George is right!

MOM: Oh, you don't mean it. *(Nudges him. He slowly walks off like a zombie.)* Now go and apologize to Susu. It isn't fair to overburden the children with your paranoid fantasies about the collapse of the dollar!

DAD: *(Turns front)* It's not a fantasy! How many days can you feed us on five dollars? How many, huh? How many *(MOM takes him by the hand, soothes him, seats him on* KATE *as chair.* DAD *delivers next speech intimately to audience.)* My great-granddad who built the railroads one tie at a time, walking all the way from Iowa to Portland, got paid a dollar a day. His room and board was twenty-five cents a week. How long can *you* eat on twenty-five cents???

MOM: *(Sits on* DOUGIE *as chair)* Oh, for heaven's sake, Dan, this is 1978.

DAD: *(Stands)* It certainly is. *(Sits again)* And that's my point.

During the next section, MOM *will sing a medley of popular love songs (from the public domain) a cappella. Choose from songs that you feel your audience will quickly identify with, and that your actress can sing and project with ease and enjoyment. This should add up to an "anti-Valentine" effect: the most seductive lyrics strung together to achieve irony. Songs important to* MOM *when she was dating* DAD, *or songs people would recognize as "love" ballads. We found we could use from two to five words of a lyric, just enough for immediate audience recognition (a la "Name That Tune"). As* MOM *sings the medley, she transforms from big band singer to torch singer to blues singer to chorus dancer, etc. The lines she* speaks *show she is clearly disturbed, but she stops this when singing.*

MOM: *(Stands, upset—speaks to herself and the audience)* I don't know how to take this. I'm as upset as Susu. *(To* DAD) When I married you, I was . . . *(she sings two to five word phrases)*

(Two kicks back and shimmy) . . . "—— —— ——." *(Alluring)*
. . . "—— —— ——." *(Helpless, arms raised above head)* "——
—— —— . . ."*(Spoken)* . . . and . . . *(Mincing steps across to* DAD*)*
"—— —— ——" the "—— —— ——." *(Cheek to cheek with* DAD*)*
"—— —— —— —— ——." *(Spoken in confidence to audience)* I
thought I had found . . . *(Throws herself over* DAD*'s lap)* "——
—— —— ——." *(Chorus line kicks across downstage)* "—— ——
—— —— ——" "—— —— —— ——." *(Spoken to audience)* And
that kept me . . . *(Hands to heart)* " . . . —— —— —— ——
——." *(Spoken)* Because . . . *(Cheesecake—hands on knees)* "——
—— —— ——." *(Reaches toward* DAD *while being blown back,
back by strong wind)* "—— —— ——," the "—— —— ——."
(Spoken) And . . . *(Perches on* DAD*'s knee, minces with shoulders)*
"—— —— —— —— ——" "—— —— —— —— ——." *(Plays
hurt, points accusing finger at* DAD *with each "You")* You—"——
—— —— ——." You—"—— —— —— —— . . ." *(Opens arms,
longing for him)* " . . . —— —— . . ." *(Plays coy, turns to side,
takes line over shoulder with foot up behind)* "—— —— ——." *(Big
sell finale)* "—— —— —— —— ——" "—— —— —— ——
—— . . ."

DAD: *(Puts hand over* MOM*'s mouth, says)* I'm old fashioned. *(He
takes her in his arms and they waltz. He sings a cappella to the tune
of "Home on the Range" as they dance.)*
I give you a home, where the microwaves roam—
Where the Speed-Queen and the Kitchen-Queen clean.
(While our little ones play.)
Where often is heard, a child's screaming words,
"I hate Mommie and Daddy," all day!
HOME, home on the Kitchen-Queen range—
Your cooking is burning each day—

Stops, looks at MOM, *who looks out at audience, aghast. They waltz
again.*

Where late, late at night
I close my eyes tight, *(Spins to left)*
And take Dolly Parton's two pies for my play. *(Spin to right)*

MOM: *(A beat, then to audience)* I'm going to run away to Alaska
with Hank Dallas. *(Turns and exits)*

All freeze, then move to next scene.

SCENE SIX

SILVER MORGAN *changes cranky to read: "Sunday Morning Before Church."* KATE *and* SUSU *remove kitchen panel from movable frame to house frame and bring bathroom panel from second story to movable frame.*

During this, DAD *drags* DOUGIE *into the bathroom for a "man to man" talk. A musical introduction to "I'm Married to Mommie" is played.* DAD *and* DOUGIE *face out, using the audience as their full-length mirror.*

DOUGIE *is unhappy—he does not want to be there. He sits and rocks.* DAD *doesn't seem to notice* DOUGIE's *actions—he is more intent on the way "he looks" and "the lesson."*

DAD: *(Stands with weight on both feet, hands on hips. Speaks to son's image in mirror.)* Now here is the way a man stands. You act like a strong man, those big boys will leave you alone.

DOUGIE *holds himself/his crotch.* DOUGIE *isn't aware that this isn't accepted.*

DAD: *(Notices* DOUGIE, *with good humor)* Now that is not quite right. *(*DOUGIE *stops touching himself and lifts one leg like a dog)* You must hold yourself like a man. That's it, that's a good idea. Yes, hitch up your pants. *(*DAD *hitches up his own pants and stands erect—*DOUGIE *follows the example)* Uh, uh, tuck in your shirt.

DOUGIE *reaches into his pants, smiles, reaches further, enjoying it. He plays with himself during* DAD's *next lines.*

DAD: No, no, it's not necessary to take off your belt. No, wait. Leave your pants on! You don't have to start all over.

DOUGIE *stops, pulls hands out of his pants and holds them up, palms forward, confused.*

DAD: Watch Daddy. *(Hitches his pants, stands straight with correct manly posture)* Now hitch them, *(*DOUG *pulls pants up to neck)* let one knee relax, *(Shifts weight—*DOUGIE *bends so far at the knee that he practically falls, as though someone hit him behind the knee)* put a tiny chip on your shoulder. *(*DOUG *hangs head with great weight on shoulder)* Just a chipmunk chip, not a whole log.

DOUGIE *straightens up. By this time he doesn't know what is expected of him. He keeps time to the music by beating his clenched fists against his thighs.*

DAD: *(Sings)* Men don't have to snarl to get respect.
N-n-n-never never bare your teeth.
My grandmother told me I looked like an animal
When I bared my teeth at my little brother.
She was right.

He notices DOUGIE's *fists, slaps* DOUGIE's *hands making him release his fists.*

DAD: *(Spoken)* You do not beat up on your sisters. No! Stop it. No! You *(Clenches his fist like old-fashioned boxer)* protect your sisters.

DOUGIE *doesn't understand. He rocks more than ever.*

DAD: *(Sings)* A man protects his sisters, his wife and his mother,
And his father when his father can no longer protect himself.
That's another important reason to have sons and to train them.
If you get off to the right start as I did,
Then you'll know how to train your son.

DAD *and* DOUGIE *do a soft-shoe dance.*

DOUGIE: *(Spoken in rhythm over music as they dance)* I'm going to marry Mommy when I grow tall.

DAD: No you're not going to marry Mommy. I'm married to Mommy.

DOUGIE: I'm going to marry Mommy and then you'll be small.

DAD: No, I'm your Daddy. I'm married to Mommy.

DOUGIE: No, she's *my* Mommy.

DAD *slaps* DOUGIE *to ground.* DOUGIE *wails.*

DAD: *(Sings)* Don't cry. *(Pulls* DOUGIE *to his feet by scruff of neck)* Don't cry. *(Twists* DOUGIE's *arm behind his back)* Men don't cry. *(Punches* DOUGIE *in stomach—*DOUGIE *doubles over but soon recovers)* If you cry, I'll make you wear your sister's clothes to school. That's right.

Hammer punch on shoulder knocks DOUGIE *to his knees.* DAD *offers hand to* DOUGIE, DOUGIE *hesitates but takes* DAD's *hand.*

DAD: Shake hands, son, I'm proud of you.

Squeezes DOUGIE's *hand hard.* DOUGIE *hurts, shakes hand to regain feeling in it.*

DAD: Now let's start again. *(Poses in mirror)* Stand like this.

Puts hands on hips, shoulders back, one foot forward. DOUGIE *is still recovering but imitates him.*

DAD: Good . . . good . . . You look cool!

They spin in opposite directions, shuffle to music with elbows out, open arms to finish.

SILVER MORGAN *announces the intermission.*

END OF ACT ONE

ACT TWO

SCENE ONE

Lights are pre-set and room panels are re-hung on house frame. The outdoor prairie panel is hung on movable frame during intermission. Cranky is turned to read: "Late Sunday night." SILVER MORGAN *runs in as a prairie dog. She makes two large running circles, sniffs, crosses to hold hand-held light on cranky. She cleans herself, calls out "Ark ark, birrrk mirk, chirk, wuf, wuf, wuf." She sniffs again, picks up scent of humans, runs off to watch from a safe vantage, holds hand-held light during song.*

While SILVER MORGAN *hides,* MOM, DAD *and* SUSU *enter. They have transformed into "The Big Kids." The little kids (*DOUGIE, JAIMIE *and* KATE) *trail after them—they are frightened and look all around.* THE BIG KIDS *are taking* THE LITTLE KIDS *on their first "snipe hunt." All search the stage armed with nets, bats, a carrot for the lure.* THE LITTLE KIDS *get underfoot—*THE BIG KIDS *make them sit in upstage R corner.*

On introduction of song, "How to Hunt a Snipe," BIG KIDS *jump and signal "Come on" to* LITTLE KIDS *three times. The fourth time they warn them with a signal to back off, to watch and stay quiet.* THE BIG KIDS *sing to each other and audience as an enticement to* THE LITTLE KIDS. *The song can be divided among the actors singing in any way the director needs—the following is the way it was done at O.M.T.* JAIMIE *accompanies song on piano.*

BIG KIDS *sing and dance.*

DAD: Hey, the air's good.

MOM & SUSU: Yeah, just right.

DAD: Ya know what I'm thinkin'?

ALL BIG KIDS: Tonight's a good night.

MOM: Air's clean, ground is tight.

SUSU: Oh, it's perfect weather.

MOM & DAD: It's perfect, it's perfect.

DAD: Duck hunters gunning.
The honkers are in flight.

MOM & SUSU: In flight, in flight, in flight.

DAD: There's one creature no hunter ever got.
That's right.

MOM & SUSU: That's hot.

ALL BIG KIDS: Ev'ry hunter's been there and back
With an Eveready flashlight and an Idaho potato sack.

DAD: But came home empty.

ALL BIG KIDS: Sunk. Skunked.

DAD: Not a single feather.
Nary a pinch of fur.

ALL BIG KIDS: Skunked!

MOM & SUSU: Ev'ry hunter's been there and back
With an Eveready flashlight and an Idaho potato sack.

MOM: Taught a lesson by Mother Nature.
In all this sportin' hype . . .

DAD: There's only one creature can do that to man.

SUSU: Yep—only one since time began.

MOM: Yep—only one critter can skunk me.

ALL BIG KIDS (*In harmony*): To the beautiful prairie Snipe!

LITTLE KIDS *become so excited they jump up and rush into the hunt, jumping and tugging on* THE BIG KIDS' *sleeves.* THE BIG KIDS *act very "cool." The following lines are spoken—*DAD, MOM *and* SUSU *are still* BIG KIDS*—*DOUGIE, JAIMIE *and* KATE *are* LITTLE KIDS.

LITTLE KIDS: (*Tugging at sleeves, pulling, begging at* BIG KIDS) Hey, what's that?

DAD: Yer too little.

LITTLE KIDS: *(Sit)* Ahhhhhh . . .

MOM & SUSU: You are, too little yet.

LITTLE KIDS: *(Pouting)* No-o-o-o-o-o-o-o-o.

BIG KIDS: *(Slapping hip pocket and extending hands)* Here's a dime— phone us when you grow up.

KATE: Come on, what animal?

SUSU: When you're old enough to know, you'll be told.

DOUGIE & JAIMIE: How old? How old?

SUSU: *(Shaking them off)* Enough.

JAIMIE: Tell us, please.

DOUGIE: Please, please tell us.

KATE: If you tell us we won't tell anyone else.

DAD: How do we know we can trust you?

ALL BIG KIDS: You hang out with girls.

LITTLE KIDS: *(To each other—they don't understand)* Our sisters.

BIG KIDS: Girls!

DOUGIE: They're good shots.

MOM: *(Collars* DOUGIE*)* That's especially why we can't tell you.

LITTLE KIDS: What? What? Why not?

SUSU: You don't get this creature with a gun.

JAIMIE: Why not?

MOM: *(Moves downstage R)* If you kill it, it disappears.

DAD: *(Moves downstage L)* Alive it's worth a billion. Any zoo will give a thousand million . . .

MOM *and* DAD *creep, backing in toward center. They bump each other and jump.*

MOM: If you bring back this hairy rarie type.

LITTLE KIDS: What is it? What?

SUSU: *(Regaining control)* Shall we tell them?

MOM & DAD: No.

LITTLE KIDS: Please, please!

SUSU: What will you give us?

JAIMIE: Our lunch, our milk money.

KATE: Our pure, unfiltered honey.

DOUGIE: Our candy, our McDonald's gift certificate.

DAD: Let's see—count it up, sonny—
Your allowance and your catcher's mitt?

DOUGIE: Yes, yes—can we go hunting for it?

DAD: You're too little, you know nothing about life,
But if you want to prove yourselves hunters of true snipe,
You have to bag and bring back alive
The one, the only . . .

LITTLE KIDS: What? What? Oh what?

BIG KIDS: *(All transform into their idea of a Snipe and jump forward)*
The Snipe!

JAIMIE *accompanies* LITTLE KIDS *on a toy xylophone as they sing.*

LITTLE KIDS: *(Sing)* What did you say?

JAIMIE: I think he said "tripe."

KATE: I think he said "ripe."

DOUGIE: I think he said "mike."

ALL LITTLE KIDS: I think he said . . .

DOUGIE: What? What did you say?

MOM: *(Jumps forward and sings as Snipe)* The Snipe!

SUSU: *(Jumps forward and sings as Snipe)* The Snipe!

DAD: *(Jumps forward and sings as Snipe)* The Snipe!

JAIMIE *returns to accompany song on piano.* DAD *and* MOM *sing
and dance as backup for* SUSU, *a la "The Supremes."*

SUSU: The true initiation,
The genuine taste of the hunt,
has to be experienced
By you runts.

DAD: No gun, no knife,
No weapon or you lose your life.

SUSU *and* DAD *transform into prairie dog mounts,* MOM *dances around them.*

MOM: 'Way 'way out on the prairie,
In the mounds of the prairie-dog town,
You have to do what no hunter has ever done—

ALL BIG KIDS: Capture a Snipe without a knife or gun.
Ev'ry hunter's been there and back
With an Eveready flashlight and an Idaho potato sack.

MOM *and* SUSU *sing and dance backup for* DAD.

DAD: You sissies, girls and dinks
Couldn't shoot a chink in a holler,
But if you bag a Snipe alive,
You can sell it for a thousand million dollars.

LITTLE KIDS: *(Spoken in awe)* A thousand million dollars?!?!?!?!?

SUSU: *(Sings)* If you brought one back alive,
They'd put you on TV and all that jive.

DAD & MOM: *(Backed up by* SUSU*)* Jimmy Carter would fly you to Mars,
Name a spaceship after you.
You'd be superstars!

LITTLE KIDS: *(Speak-sing with* JAIMIE *on xylophone)* Here's the place to hunt them.

KATE *produces a large sack,* DOUGIE *a soft-sculpture carrot. They set it up center stage as a trap for the Snipe.*

LITTLE KIDS: Coax it in the sack.
Turn on the light,
Hide! Get back!

KATE *puts carrot in bag.* LITTLE KIDS *hide.*

BIG KIDS: *(As they creep off to hide—*LITTLE KIDS *freeze)* Be very still. If you move, the Snipe will kill!

They turn back as though they have exited, peer back over their shoulders.

LITTLE KIDS: *(Excited, tiptoeing off to hide)* Without a gun, Without a knife.
The time is ripe.

JAIMIE *plays alluring Snipe music on xylophone.* SILVER MORGAN *enters, liking the music, and looks around.* LITTLE KIDS *are deliciously frightened.* SILVER *pounces on bag, attracted by carot, finally crawls into the bag.* LITTLE KIDS *rush in and tie bag tight—*SILVER MORGAN *is caught and struggles.*

LITTLE KIDS: Yippee!!! We've snared a Snipe!

BIG KIDS *jump forward, shocked, then exit by turning their backs.*

KATE *lifts bag to her shoulders,* JAIMIE *and* DOUGIE *help.*

ALL: *(Sing—*LITTLE KIDS *carrying the bagged "Snipe")*
With an Eveready flashlight
And an Idaho potato sack!

Freeze, then move to next scene.

SCENE TWO

DAD *moves to cranky and changes it to read: "Monday Evening Before Dad Gets Home."* KATE *moves the movable frame to the side of the playing area—the following family-room scene is played in front of all house panels.*

The bagged "Snipe" (SILVER MORGAN) *hops around the family room.* MOM, SUSU, DOUGIE, KATE *and* JAIMIE *are looking out window for* DAD. *(At O.M.T. they transformed into a radar scanner trying to pick up* DAD, *moving and looking right, then left, as a group.)* SUSU *leaves this activity to try to contain the "Snipe."*

SUSU: *(Struggles with Snipe bag, still trying to see out window)* Is he coming down the walk?

DOUGIE: *(Breaks from group, looks out window)* Just pulled into the drive.

SUSU: I don't know how long I can keep it in here.

DOUGIE: You better keep it in there, or it might kill you.

SUSU: It'll kill you first. *(Pushes bag toward him)*

KATE: Stop that. Don't fight when we have such a big surprise for Dad. *(Takes bag, calms it)*

MOM: *(Spraying to rid the house of odor)* That's right. I've always wanted more animals around our place. If this works out, maybe we can start a herd of Nubian goats.

CHILDREN *transform into goats and bleat.* DOUGIE *tries to join in.*

JAIMIE: *(Hugs MOM, who keeps deodorizing)* Oh Mama, oh please, can we? Can we? *(DOUGIE stares out window)*

MOM: This has to work out first.

JAIMIE: But we don't know how to train it.

MOM: Your father will. He trained animals for the rodeo when he was young.

KATE: *(Looking at bag, running and hanging on MOM)* I bet this is the biggest one in the whole world.

MOM: Bet it's the only one.

DOUGIE: *(Crosses to MOM)* Millions of people have been Snipe hunting, but no one ever caught one before.

JAIMIE, KATE *and* DOUGIE *are hanging on* MOM *like baby monkeys.*

MOM: I'm gonna call the Omaha Herald *(or local newspaper)*

KATE: No—people will get jealous.

MOM: Let's ask Dad.

SUSU: *(With "Snipe")* People see somthing rare as a Snipe, they might kill it. *All* KIDS *transform into spectacular death images, then fall)*

KATE: *(Breaks out of image—all transform back to themselves, shake hands)* We have to protect it.

DOUGIE: *(Coming forward)* They'd think it was an alien.

JAIMIE: *(Behind him, coming forward)* It could be an alien!

DOUGIE: *(He and* JAIMIE *holding each other)* Yes, it could, it might kill us.

SUSU: *(Upstage L of bag looking at it)* It wouldn't!

KATE: *(Upstage R of bag looking at it)* It has such a sweet smile.

DOUGIE: *(Joins* SUSU *to left of bag, scared)* But sharp teeth.

KATE: You have sharp teeth.

DOUGIE: You have a sharp tongue.

SUSU: *(Bravely holds bag and calms it)* Sure it has sharp teeth—it's been gnawing on roots like the other prairie dogs.

JAIMIE: *(Kisses* MOM*)* Will the mother dog miss it?

KATE: Sure.

JAIMIE: *(Runs away from* MOM*)* Mama, would you miss me . . . *(From across stage, starts to approach* MOM, *making a giant opening-and-closing mouth with her arms)* . . . if some giants came and took me home with them?

MOM: No.*(Pretends to faint)*

JAIMIE: *(Sits)* Mama!

MOM: *(Pops back up, opens arms to* JAIMIE*)* Of course I'd miss you. Wouldn't you miss us?

JAIMIE: Maybe.

MOM: Maybe?

JAIMIE: I'd be too busy eating giant food. *(Approaches* KATE *and* DOUGIE, *again making giant mouth with arms)*

SUSU: *(Hears sounds from bag)* Oh, oh, it wants out.

MOM: *(Dusting)* Did you make the air holes?

SUSU: Um . . . uh . . . it's been living underground with the prairie dogs. It could go without air for two or three weeks.

DOUGIE: You're crazy.

KATE: Not crazy—stupid.

JAIMIE: *(Notices through window that* DAD *is coming, jumps with excitement)* Here he comes, here he comes!!

SUSU: (KIDS *try to hide the bagged "Snipe")* Quick, get in front. Hide it, hide it. *(They overdo their protective stances)*

KATE: *(Looking around)* Act normal! *(They relax)*

SUSU: I can, but you can't. You're crazy as a girl.

KATE: We're both girls, you cow pie!

MOM: *(Dusting)* Be nice, or we'll have to set the creature free.

DAD *enters exhausted. He carries a soft-sculpture newspaper.*

DAD: *(To audience)* Oh boy, oh boy. *(To family)* Oh, hello you guys. I'm pooped.

SUSU: Hi Dad.

KATE: Hi Dad.

JAIMIE: Hi Dad.

DOUGIE: Hi Dad!

DAD *opens his arms to his son, they wrestle, the other kids cheer.* DAD *pins* DOUGIE, *triumphant.*

MOM: *(Bending over for kiss)* Hi dear.

DAD: *(Kiss)* Hi dear.

MOM: Have a good day?

DAD *releases* DOUGIE. *The* GIRLS *push* DOUGIE *and* SILVER MORGAN *(in bag), transforming them into* DAD's *recliner.* DAD *picks up newspaper and relaxes in recliner.*

DAD: Rotten! G.L.P.X. bought our company.

MOM: What?

DAD: *(To* KIDS, *who gather around him,* MOM *sitting at his feet)* Come here and give your old man a hug.

MOM: Dear?

DAD: Your old man may be out of a job.

MOM: *(Stroking* DAD's *feet)* But why? But why? You're good. *(Looks straight ahead)* You go to work every day, even in the blizzards. When the tornado hit, you went to work.

DAD: *(Rises)* G.L.P.X. is looking at each one of us very carefully. *(Fencing lunge)* Half the executives got canned today. *(Still fencing, jumps back from an attack)* We don't know who's next. Pour me a drink!!! (MOM *dashes off to get it)* My hand's shaking.

MOM: *(Returning with drink)* Darling, should we discuss this in front of the children?

DAD: They might as well know what a rat-race, cutthroat world it is out there. (CHILDREN *transform into terror-street images)*

Noises from the bagged "Snipe." KIDS *make noise to cover it up.* DAD *hears noises,* KATE *jumps on his back and kisses him as a distraction.*

KATE: We love you, Daddy.

MOM: We love you.

SUSU: We have a present for you.

JAIMIE: It's the only one in captivity.

DOUGIE: We looked in the *Guiness Book of Records.*

KATE: No one else ever brought one back alive before.

SUSU *sits on floor, knees up, arms open. Each child sits on the knees of the speaker before. This should look like the* CHILDREN *made up an "act" for* DAD.

SUSU: We have—

JAIMIE & KATE: —a big—

ALL KIDS: *SURPRISE! (All open knees so all fall on floor—they laugh)* —for you.

Stage directions for the following speech were used at O.M.T. These can be used or not as the director sees fit.

DAD: *(Picks up paper, takes line over his shoulder to the audience)* Let me have a drink and read the paper and take my nap before dinner. *(Over other shoulder)* I can't stomach any more surprises. *(Turns his back to the audience, jumps over the paper and bends over—he speaks to the audience through his legs, the paper extended up over his back—he struggles with this, as the news is burdensome)* This all happened between ten and eleven Eastern time to our Company. When we working stiffs got the news, it was dinner hour and I couldn't eat—none of us could eat. *(Stands up, faces audience)* I don't have a department any more. *(Extends arm)* They left me my file clerk. *(Relaxes arm from wrist to elbow—it dangles)* I'm supposed to learn to type. *(Both arms extended to sides—force pulls him back and forth)* They requisitioned my secretary for the Chicago office. *(Big circles back with arms, slap back pockets)* She knows everything, *everything.* She's the only one who knows where everything is. She's a goldmine! *(Rises)* I'm sorry, dear Lord, I ever asked her to comb her hair. *(Stands, head bowed)* I'm sorry, dear Lord, for yelling at her to replace her lipstick after lunch. *(Arms and head extended up in prayer)* I'm sorry, dear Lord, for making her bring me and Bill coffee eight times a day with three sugars and heavy on the cream. *(To audience and self)* Even if I stay, I'll have to fake it, until we . . . here, honey *(Hands her glass),* another. Make it a double.

MOM: But you never drink except at Christmas and New Year's.

DAD: *(Holds her against his chest)* I'm gonna get bombed. What's the difference now? Nothing's the same. What good is our bomb shelter?

MOM: *(Spinning around, confused)* Darling?

DAD: What good is our bomb shelter?

MOM: *(Stops spinning)* Why it's a perfect bomb shelter, darling. I could use it for all our home canning—if I knew how to can.

DAD: *(Sends MOM off)* You get on the phone to your mother, and get instructions. We're going to tighten our belts around her. *(KIDS transform to "tighten belt" image)* No more McDonald's. *(KIDS gasp)*

KATE: No—

JAIMIE: —more—

DOUGIE: —Mc—

SUSU: —Donald's?!

CHILDREN: *(Plead)* Oh Dad, oh Dad, please . . .

DAD: No more McDonald's. You'll learn to cook!

CHILDREN: *(Gather around him pleading, pulling at him)* Oh Dad, oh Dad!

DAD: Get to the kitchen. Your mother will give you your first lesson. *(Sends GIRLS to kitchen)* And don't use the microwave. We'll sell it.

MOM: *(Rushing back)* Not the microwave! *(Kneels pleading at his feet)*

DAD: Sell it! *(She jumps)*

MOM: *(Tiptoes around him)* Darling, this isn't like you. You usually have such a positive attitude.

DAD: *(Triumphant, pushes her to floor)* I still have a positive attitude! *(Raises arm in triumph, one foot on MOM)* I'm a survivor. We don't need low-grade radiation. Get rid of the television sets too.

CHILDREN: *(As a means of pleading with DAD, they try everything— melodramatic images of pain, sorrow, deprivation)* Not that! Anything but that! Don't sell the TV!

DAD: *(Crosses upstage, comes back downstage moving through pleading KIDS)* All you do is play pong on it anyway. Back to basics! Set up the old wooden ping-pong table in the garage. I'll sell two of the cars and all the minibikes.

CHILDREN: *(Continue pleading actions)* Not that, not that!

SUSU: I just got my driver's license!

DAD: You will learn to walk. *(They transform into themselves as babies taking a difficult first step)* All of you! Maybe adversity is a good thing. The way you kids been going you soon won't have any arms or legs at all—just flippers *(KIDS transform to a favorite mechanical toy)* like on your electronic pinball game. *(Signals* MOM, *who rushes out)* Bring me a triple! I like feeling better. This is good. If I can't be an executive at work, I can certainly be one in my own home.

JAIMIE: *(Run to* DAD*)* But Daddy, don't you want to see . . .

KATE: *(Runs to* DAD*)* We have this great present for you . . .

DAD: Take it back *(They imagine a slap—and fall in unison)* and bring me the cash. No more sentiment till we get back on our feet.

MOM: *(Hanging on* DAD*'s shoulder)* But dear, *you* didn't get a pink slip.

DAD: *(Forces* MOM *to her knees, sits on her shoulders)* Even if they do keep me on, they might decrease my salary.

MOM: Then quit.

DAD: What? *(Jumps up)*

MOM: Quit. Beat them to it.

DAD: Quit? *(Helps* MOM *to her feet)*

MOM: *(Speaks word syllable by syllable)* Resign. (DAD *mouths word slowly)*

DAD: Quitters never win, and winners never quit!

MOM: *(Pulls his head to her bosom)* Don't let them make you feel bad. Who do they think they are?

DAD: They've been paying our salary for twenty years, that's who they are.

MOM: We're not stupid. We're Americans. We can do any-thing. We can go into business for ourselves. (CHILDREN *transform into a fast-food hamburger machine operator, a computer programmer, etc.)*

DAD: With what capital?

MOM: The money we've been saving to send the kids to college.

CHILDREN: *(Transform to cheerleaders)* Hooray—no more school!

DAD: *(Drops to hands and knees, whispers at audience)* You're crazy! *(Repeats line crawling across front of stage while children cheer)*

MOM: Anyway they'd make more money as electricians or plumbers.

SUSU: *(Transforms into a trucker)* I can make twenty-five thousand a year driving a semi.

DAD: My kids are going to work with their head, not their hands. *(Grabs SUSU's head, pulls it back, releases it—all KIDS transform into dolls with heads that wiggle back and forth, side to side.)*

The giant bag begins to hop around the room.

DAD: *(Runs, hides behind MOM)* What's that? What the hell is that? I haven't had that much to drink! Where's my gun?

SUSU: No no, Dad.

CHILDREN: No no, Dad.

SUSU: That's your surprise.

DAD: *(Holding on to MOM)* It's alive? *(Kneels)* Oh my God—not another mouth to feed!

SUSU: It's the only one in captivity.

KATE: We captured it. *(Picks up SUSU and holds her like a rifle—JAIMIE helps)*

DAD: What is it?

KATE: We went hunting.

JAIMIE: The big boys on the corner showed us how.

SUSU: They went out at midnight with a lantern and a gunny sack and went out to the prairie dog village, and inside of an hour they had captured the Snipe. *(KATE puts her down)*

DOUGIE: *(Teasing bag with carrot—the "Snipe" (SILVER MORGAN) goes after him)* It loves carrots and flowers. The big boys ran away when they saw we had something alive in the sack.

GIRLS *take the bag from* DOUGIE.

DAD: Alive? I know you mean well,but Daddy's loading his gun in case.

KATE: *(Picks up bag—other* KIDS *help)* It's a Snipe.

JAIMIE: But *(Whispers and giggles)* it thinks it's a prairie dog.

KATE: It's been living with prairie dogs all its life.

DOUGIE: It's a hundred times bigger than a prairie dog, but it doesn't know it.

SUSU: It's so cute—wait till you see its face.

JAIMIE: Oh it's so cute—we thought you'd love it.

KATE: We love it.

DOUGIE: Don't shoot.

SUSU: *(*CHILDREN *get in front of "Snipe" and protect it with their bodies)* You'll have to shoot us first.

DAD: Mutiny! In my own house! *(To* MOM *on hands and knees)* Why did you bring up my children to be so independent?

CHILDREN *make a pyramid, "Snipe" hops through it.*

MOM: Oh, stop yelling. You're going to love it, Dan.

DAD: Love it! I'm going to kill it!

SILVER MORGAN *wriggles out of bag, jumps up on* DAD, *knocks him down, sits on his chest and kisses his face.* DAD *yells with fright at first, then begins to like it.* KIDS *are thoroughly enjoying it.*

DOUGIE: Shall I get the gun, Dad? Shall I? Shall I?

DAD: No, not yet!

As SILVER MORGAN *throws her head back, all freeze, then move to next scene.*

SCENE THREE

SUSU *changes cranky to read: "Monday at Midnight."* DOUGIE *is alone with* SILVER MORGAN *in the family room.* DOUGIE *puts "Snipe" cage on movable frame and brings it center stage, the family room.* SILVER MORGAN *hops in and kisses at* DOUGIE, *who sits and rocks right of cage.* SILVER MORGAN *makes up to* DOUGIE, *barking, chirping and kissing at him.*

DOUGIE: I don't like you. My Mama and my sisters love animals. *(Stops rocking)* They should—they *are* animals. *(Rocks)* I've looked all over inside my head, and I don't feel close to you at all—and I don't feel bad about it either. You have great big eyes like Bambi. But you know something? *(Teases* SILVER MORGAN *with carrot, then bites it himself)* I hate Bambi. *(Standing)* If you can't fly out of the forest when there's a forest fire, too bad for you. *(Flying saint image)* I can fly. I can fly two or three feet at a time. I could fly farther, but I'm saving my energy. *(Sits and rocks)* They think I won't talk to them because I'm mad at Dad, but I'm not. He's a puny flop. I'm saving *my* energy. *(Rocks)* He wastes his. I'm going to find God. *(Glares at* SILVER MORGAN*)* Every time I look at you I want to poke you with a stick. *(Moves away)* You sure are hairy and dirty. Why do you smile all the time? You're locked up. *(Stands)* You're *bad!* You don't fool me. I bet you want to wiggle your way into a good bed and three meals a day here. *(Stuffs carrot in his mouth, rattles cage)* But guess what? You came too late *(Picks up imaginary jar)* There's only one spoonful left in the peanut butter jar. *(Scoops peanut butter with carrot)* How are you going to split *that* seven ways?

Both freeze, then move to next scene.

SCENE FOUR

SUSU *changes cranky to read: "Tuesday at Dawn." The scene is still the family room.* SILVER MORGAN *is asleep in her cage.* SUSU, KATE *and* JAIMIE *sneak up on the cage, each from a different corner of the playing area.*

JAIMIE: Are you going to let "it" out of the cage?

KATE & SUSU: *(As they creep)* Shhhhhh, Jaimie!

KATE: "Her."

JAIMIE: Are you going to let "her" out?

SUSU: *(Pulls* JAIMIE *away from cage)* I'd love to, but she'd run away.

JAIMIE: Shouldn't we let her go back to her mommy?

KATE: If we knew who her mommy was.

JAIMIE: Why, her mommy lives in the ground like she did. *(Makes a cave of* KATE's *body and hides)*

KATE: Her mommy isn't a prairie dog.

JAIMIE: It is too. We saw her mommy.

KATE: *(Pause—*KATE *and* SUSU *look at each other as if to say "The kid's nuts")* If we saw her mommy, we wouldn't have captured her.

SUSU: You saw her mommy?

JAIMIE: *(Transforms into a prairie dog)* She had whiskers. She stood up on her paws and cried and cried when you put the Snipe in the bag.

KATE: Imagination!

JAIMIE: I did see her!

SUSU: *(Stroking* JAIMIE's *hair)* I know you feel for her mommy, but we don't know who her mommy is. Maybe she thinks the prairie dog is her mommy and the other prairie dogs are her brothers and sisters. But she's a girl, like us, and she should know it.

JAIMIE: Why?

KATE: She should know she's a girl and then she can be like us.

JAIMIE: *(As prairie dog)* But wouldn't it be more fun if *we* were prairie dogs? We'd get to dig in the ground all the time, and live safe and warm. Nobody gets mad if you get dirty, because dirt is home.

SILVER MORGAN *rolls over, reminding girls that she's sleeping.* KATE *and* SUSU *grab* JAIMIE. *Swing her in their arms to calm her.*

SUSU: It's four o'clock in the morning. You're going to wake up Daddy.

JAIMIE: *(Gasps, backs off)* I don't want to wake up Daddy!

KATE: Do you want to help us teach her to talk?

JAIMIE: Why?

KATE *and* SUSU *pick* JAIMIE *up and rock her in joined arms through the next lines.*

KATE: We had to teach *you* to talk.

JAIMIE: Mama said I talked at six months, and none of you talked till you were two.

SUSU: We loved you so much and played with you and talked to you so that you talked early.

JAIMIE: I was born talking. (KATE *and* SUSU *drop her and give each other a look)*

KATE: Susu, make her help or send her to bed!

SUSU: (JAIMIE *clings to her)* Jaimie, if you want to help, pay attention and don't argue.

JAIMIE: I just like to think of other ways to be and . . . O.K. O.K. I'll teach her the A-B-C song. *(Crosses to cage, sits and sings "A-B-C")*

SUSU: *(She and* KATE *sigh, give each other "the look")* First we have to gain her confidence. Let's try to talk like *she* does.

JAIMIE: *(Jumps up)* Yippee! That's what I meant before. *(Becomes prairie dog)* I want to talk Prairie Dog. Let's all live underground—then we won't have to wash windows or worry about the energy crisis.

SUSU *and* KATE *"give look" to each other.* JAIMIE *transforms into a digging, yipping prairie dog.*

KATE: Don't get carried away. *(Jive-strut next line in rhythm)* Listen to Susu, and do what we do.

KATE *and* SUSU *choose an activity that will divert* JAIMIE's *attention—at O.M.T. they formed "Choo-Choo Train" and circled playing area.*

SUSU: If we teach the Snipe to talk, Mom and Daddy may let us keep her.

JAIMIE: To live with us forever?

KATE: Until she gets married.

JAIMIE: What if she doesn't like us?

SUSU: If you show love, she'll give it back. *(Goes for a closer look at* SILVER)

KATE: *(To* SUSU) How are we going to teach her?

SUSU: At school they showed this film about how they taught babies to talk in an orphanage. They listened to the babies, and imitated the sounds the babies made—then when the babies thought they had learned baby language, they taught the babies English by imitation and association—Follow the Leader!

Follow-the-Leader game continues through SUSU's *speech, with* SUSU *leading,* KATE *and* JAIMIE *following.* JAIMIE *repeats "ear" each time* SUSU *says it, points to her own ear.*

KATE: What's association?

SUSU: When they'd wash a baby's ear, *(Puts fingers in her ear and twists—*KATE *and* JAIMIE *follow)* just at the moment they'd put the washcloth on the baby's ear to clean it, they would say "ear." *(Hands out)* They did this until the baby made the connection between the sound and its own ear. The baby learned that the word "ear" meant its own ear.

JAIMIE: *(Jumps up, stopping game)* Are we going to wash the Snipe?

SUSU: When we gain her confidence.

KATE: She sure smells.

SUSU: Don't show that you don't like the smell. It's *her* smell and it smells good to her. *(All smell and show they like it)*

JAIMIE: *(Sniffs as a prairie dog)* Smells good to me too. I love smells. *(Rolls in dirt)*

KATE: *(Crosses to* JAIMIE, *covers her mouth)* For Pete's sake, chatter box! I'm going to put *you* in the cage when the Snipe comes out.

SUSU: Now look. We have to work as a team. We have to do everything together so the Snipe doesn't get confused.

JAIMIE: *(Stands by* SUSU *and does everything she does)* I'm on the team.

KATE: Shouldn't we give her a name?

SUSU: *(Nods)* I hate calling her Snipe. Especially since no such thing exists. (JAIMIE *nods in imitation)*

JAIMIE: *(Crosses to cage—pause)* I'm going to name her Jaimie Junior.

SUSU: That's a warm thought, but everyone should have a chance to offer names.

KATE: She sure is hairy. Shouldn't we cut her hair and wash her?

SUSU: I don't think so—not till she trusts us.

JAIMIE: Would she bite me?

SUSU: She seems to be more into kissing than biting. (JAIMIE *transforms into prairie dog and jumps, sniffs and kisses at* SUSU)

KATE: That's how prairie dogs greet each other. They can tell by the taste and smell of each other's breath who belongs in their family.

JAIMIE: *(Turns out, wipes mouth)* Oooooooooooo, I don't want her to kiss me. She has sharp teeth.

SUSU: She's gentle, and if she wants to kiss you, you let her. Are you on the team or not?

JAIMIE: I'm on the team. (KATE *and* SUSU *give "look" to each other that conveys "Is this a good idea?")*

KATE: What do we do?

SUSU *signals to others. She and* JAIMIE *sit up right of cage,* KATE *up left, they creep like spiders on hands and feet.*

SUSU: Let's sit near her. Creep very carefully, don't make any sudden moves. When she wakes up, imitate any sound she makes. Try to hold eye contact. Imitate any movement she makes.

JAIMIE: *(Stands)* What if she goes to the bathroom?

SUSU: Pretend to do it too. *(Creeps around cage)* I've never been so excited in my life. *(Gets so excited she forgets to creep)* If we can teach her to talk we'll have the best 4-H exhibit at the State Fair! We could even try to teach it better than we were taught. I believe we should try to do that.

KATE: How will we know it's better?

SUSU: *(Signals to others—they all huddle)* We'll have to think of a way we can teach her to talk without making her feel that being a girl is not as good as being a boy.

KATE: Impossible with Dad and Doug around!

JAIMIE: Especially Dougie *(Crosses to look at SILVER still asleep)*

SUSU: We have to win them over.

KATE: Take my advice and don't tell them anything.

JAIMIE: *(Laughs, points, jumps)* Her ear moved. *(All move to back of cage to look at SILVER MORGAN)*

KATE: She's human—her ear can't move.

JAIMIE: I can move my ears. *(Sits in front of cage and tries to wiggle her ears)*

KATE: *(Reaches out, clutches hands with SUSU)* Do you really think we can do this with You-Know-Who "helping"?

SUSU: *(Both jump forward and make solidarity fist)* I want to try. Women have got to get it together, and *(Arm around KATE)* if we can't do it in our own home, where can we?

KATE: I don't think You-Know-Who is old enough.

JAIMIE: I am too old enough. *(Looks around KATE's legs—breaks through)*

SUSU: It's not just a scientific experiment with the Snipe, but to see if we can learn to work as a team. Boys do it all the time.

KATE: All right.

They make a pact—sandwich stack of one hand at a time—then move stack up and down two times.

SUSU: Smile when you say that. *(Arms up and down again—all break, smiling. Signals them to creep again. They start from original places.)* O.K., creep closer to the cage. *(They do)*

SILVER MORGAN *yawns and rolls over. They jump back, terrified, then recover. They imitate her yawn and roll. She yawns and rolls over again. They jump back again, then imitate her, yawn and roll over forward. She sits up, smacks lips, throws kisses, opens eyes and makes hugging gestures at them.* KATE *and* JAIMIE *jump back, but* SUSU *isn't frightened any more. All hug and kiss at* SILVER MORGAN. SILVER MORGAN *watches them, claps hands, barks, yips and kisses at them. They imitate her.*

KATE: *(Jumping, kissing and hugging with* SUSU*)* Hey, Susu!

SUSU: Don't talk.

KATE: Hey, I think she digs us.

SUSU: Bark!

KATE: Is this communication?

SUSU: *(Stops)* Not quite. *(Pause)*

They go back to imitating SILVER MORGAN, *who makes gurgling sounds.* SILVER MORGAN *sees something in cage, picks it up, moves with cage. As* GIRLS *are in a line across the stage,* SILVER MORGAN *pretends to be looking at something else.*

KATE: *(Sotto voce, while imitating* SILVER MORGAN*)* Susu, she's looking at something. *(Gurgling)* What should we do?

SUSU: Just keep trying to imitate her sounds and gestures.

SILVER MORGAN *makes laughing sound, and while looking in opposite direction, throws soft-sculpture piece of dirt at* JAIMIE.

JAIMIE: *(Jumps forward)* Ahhhhhhhhhhhhh! SUSU! She threw doo-doo at me. *(Attacks, shaking Snipe cage)* Poooo-ooooohhhh, dirty, bad, bad, bad!

SUSU: *(She and* KATE *grab* JAIMIE, *hold her aloft)* Hush, hush, you'll ruin it. Don't wake up the house.

JAIMIE: *(Wriggles free, looks at herself)* Doo-doo all over my jammies. Doo-doo!

KATE: *(Rolls eyes)* Oh my God.

SUSU: Don't swear. *(To* JAIMIE, *calming)* It is not—it's only nice clean dirt from her old home.

JAIMIE *takes the "doo-doo" and throws it back at* SILVER MORGAN.

SUSU: Hey!

JAIMIE: You said to do what she did. *(Points at* SILVER MORGAN, *laughs)* Look—she likes it. She's kissing at me! *(Kisses back)*

SUSU: We have to start all over again.

JAIMIE: *(Keeps kissing)* No. She's kissing at me.

KATE: *(Sotto voce, kissing back)* Kiss back, stupid.

SUSU: Don't call names. We're starting over.

KATE: Starting over what?

SUSU: A way to be.

KATE: Sorry. *(More kisses at* SILVER MORGAN*)*

SILVER MORGAN *kisses and barks, all kiss and bark, volume increases.*

KATE: Hey, Susu, this is getting loud.

SUSU: Try barking quieter than she does, and see if we can bring it down.

They do. The bark sounds more like "chirk" than "woof." SILVER MORGAN *folds arms on chest, bares teeth at girls, makes kissing sounds then three barks, comes up to bars of cage and catches* JAIMIE *by skirt, holds her by hips, strokes her hair through bars.* JAIMIE *yells, but* SILVER MORGAN *kisses her.*

JAIMIE: *(Squirms, scared)* Susu . . .

SUSU: Smile—we're getting somewhere.

SUSU *imitates* SILVER MORGAN's *grooming of* JAIMIE *with* KATE.

KATE: *(To* SUSU*)* Your breath isn't so hot.

SUSU: *(Sotto voce)* If you can't say anything nice . . .

KATE: I know, I know. Hey, she's smiling.

JAIMIE: *(Tries to keep smiling)* Her nails are sharp. I want to go back to bed.

SUSU: Are you too little?

JAIMIE: *(Slow admission)* Maybe.

KATE: Quitters never win and winners never quit.

JAIMIE: I ain't no quitter.

KATE: Then kiss back.

JAIMIE: Mush.

SUSU: It's not mush to prairie dogs—it means hello.

JAIMIE: Blah.

KATE: *(Crosses, pries* JAIMIE *from* SILVER MORGAN *and takes her place)* I'll do it.

JAIMIE: *(Runs to* SUSU, *shows arm)* I'm not quitting. But look at my arm. See the scratches.

SUSU: They'll heal. Come on—do what I do. *(Hugs* JAIMIE *around hips, pats and strokes her hair)*

SILVER MORGAN, KATE, SUSU *and* JAIMIE *sing and dance a chanting lullaby.*

JAIMIE:	SUSU:	KATE & SILVER:
Chirk, chirk-a-girk,		*(Kiss)* Chirk chirk,
Birk, mirk-a-girk	Chirk-a-girk,	*(Kiss)* Chirk chirk,
Hark, hark-a-gark		*(Kiss)* Mirk mirk,
ark ark.	Hark-a-gark,	*(Kiss)* Quirk quirk,
Wuff, wuff-a-tuff		*(Kiss)* Rip lip,
Ruff, tuff-a-stuff	Mirk-a-birk . . .	*(Kiss)* Skip trip . . .
Whirr . . .		

Lullaby is sung through twice, accompanied by hugging, stroking and kissing. The second time SILVER MORGAN *ends with a howl, "Ahhh!" brought on by* KATE'S *catching a tangle of her hair.* DAD *and* DOUGIE *bound in to see what's wrong.*

DAD: What the hell's going on here?!?

DOUGIE: Oh my God, they're kissing. Oh how gross! *(Sits downstage and starts rocking)*

—DAD *picks up feather duster, waves it in air like weapon, approaching* SILVER MORGAN *in cage.*

KATE: *(Caressing* SILVER MORGAN*)* It's all right. Birk chirk. Rick mick whirr chirk.

DAD: *(Hitting at cage)* Let go, Katie—it could give you rabies!

KATE: Hush, Dad.

SUSU: *(Pulls at* DAD'S *waist)* Dad, don't—you'll ruin everything.

DAD: *(Keeps swinging at* SILVER MORGAN*)* You're going crazy, barking and drooling! What's happening to my life?

DOUGIE: *(Stands, pulls up pants, jumps)* Shall I get the gun, Dad? Shall I? Shall I?

SUSU: You stay where you are, Doug.

DOUGIE: *(Makes ritual sign of the cross in every corner of the playing area)* The Snipe's put a spell on them.

SUSU: Hush up.

DAD: *(Trying to shake* SUSU *off)* Let go, damn it. That's it. I'm calling the cops. *(*JAIMIE *runs to stop him)*

SUSU: You might say that.

DAD: Get back! Get back! *(To* SILVER MORGAN*)* Into your bed! Lay down!

KATE: *(Flings arms around* DAD*)* Don't treat her like a dog.

DAD: It's wild. God knows what diseases it's carrying.

DOUGIE: I'll get the gun in case. *(He starts out—*KATE *trips him)*

KATE: Stay here, Dougie. *(Pulls him up by neck—*JAIMIE *puts her hand over his mouth)* Dad might need your help.

DAD: *(Picks* JAIMIE *up, notices her arm)* Jaimie. What's on your arm? Blood?

JAIMIE: *(Looks at her sisters, who hold their breath, looks at* SILVER MORGAN, *then at* DAD*)* I drew on my arm with my red pen. *(Sisters sigh)*

SUSU: Dad, we're trying to teach her to talk.

DAD: I can't take any more shocks. We're going to call the Henry Doorly Zoo and have them come and get her. *(KATE shrieks)* Don't wake your mother.

SUSU *is deep in thought.*

KATE: You can't do it, you can't do it, you can't. We love her.

JAIMIE: We want to name her.

KATE: She's ours—we found her.

DOUGIE: I did too. I bagged her.

KATE: We both did—we were both pulling the bag tight. You couldn't do it alone. *(To DAD)* I want to keep her.

SUSU: Dad, you don't want to lose out on a great opportunity. We could contribute a lot to scientific knowledge if we make contact and bring her out of the animal stage.

DAD: To the zoo!

SUSU: *(Pleading on knees)* Dad, you can't put her in the zoo.

DAD: Just watch me.

SUSU: The zoo's for animals.

DAD: So?

SUSU: This is a human being.

SILVER MORGAN *makes kissing sounds and brushes back her hair. She poses like a model, pulls hair up on top of head.*

JAIMIE: *(Pulling cage left, then down center)* Look, look. If she had a bath and a bathing suit, the Snipe would look like Miss America.

DOUGIE: What a gross-out! *(Sits and rocks)*

KATE: *(Looks at SILVER MORGAN)* She's . . . she's different . . .

SUSU: She's beautiful. She's perfect. Come on, everyone. Imitate her. *(Girls imitate SILVER MORGAN)*

DAD: Imitate . . . a wild animal?

SUSU: Dad, we almost had her talking and singing. *(Tries*

seduction tactic like MOM—*throws herself on his shoulder)* Please do it for me . . . just try, just once, Dad. Oh please, Dad. *(Eye to eye—pulls his face down to hers)* We used to be pals . . . won't you just try for me, your first old pal?

DAD: Don't try to butter me.

KATE: *(Crosses to* DAD*)* Dad, if we can talk with her we could make a lot of money. I bet we could make a *lot* of money.

JAIMIE: *(Takes* SILVER MORGAN, *still in cage, by the hand)* We could take her to school and sell tickets to let everyone kiss her.

DOUGIE: Arggggg arggggggg. Oh, no. *(Holds throat, chokes, falls over in tantrum)*

KATE: We could sell the story of her and us to *The Enquirer.*

DAD: That rotten supermarket newspaper?

SUSU: They pay twenty-five thousand and up for good stories.

DAD: *(Turns quickly, surprised)* They don't.

SUSU: They do. *(Imitates* SILVER MORGAN *and does a "Miss America" turn)*

DAD: *(Kicking* DOUGIE *to his feet)* Twenty-five thousand! *(Muses)* Miss America . . .

SILVER MORGAN *barks and prances, brushes and tosses her hair, stands on her toes, crosses arms on her chest, uncrosses arms and waves at them, prances, kisses and barks. Whole family imitates her.* DOUGIE *starts to laugh, but* DAD *mutters and makes him join them.* JAIMIE *goes to piano.*

DAD: *(Sings and dances)* Get the camera, get the flash.
We have to document this to make our stash
Of cash.

SUSU: Hey, Dad,
It'll be too bad
If we don't get this down on paper.

DAD: We have to name her.
A name's important, will help to tame her.

All fall into "thinking" poses.

DOUGIE: *(Jumps up, rock)* Let's name her Honey—
Honey Money!

JAIMIE: No, let's name her Goldilocks.

DOUGIE: Let's name her Moldy.

DAD: Let's name her Cash.

SUSU: Stop that holler!

KATE: Let's name her Morgan Silver Dollar.
Let's name her Silver Morgan.

SUSU: I want to run and tell:
Her name is Silver Morgan Connell!

DAD: Here's the camera—be sure to hold it steady.
We want perfect pictures when our story's ready.

SUSU: We have to get this all down in order.
I'm gonna turn on the tape recorder.

SILVER MORGAN: *(Comes out of Snipe cage)*
Eeny meeny miney moe,
Catch a pronoun by the toe.
If she hollers make her say
"I was born in the U.S.A."

MOM *rushes in with room deoderizer*—SILVER MORGAN *lunges back to the safety of her cage.*

MOM: *(Spoken)* What's happening?

Piano plays "I'm Married to Mommy" under the following spoken lines.

SUSU: Mama, our new life's begun. We'll teach her English.

MOM: Can't we start over? *(To DAD and DOUGIE)* What are *you* doing? You look like bathing cuties.

DAD: This is cash on the line, Mother. I'm quitting my job. *(Spins her around)* We'll get a camper. *(To DOUGIE)* Get that shot. Have you got it? Get it again. *(MOM strikes poses with spray can, thinking she's the one being photographed)* Wow, it feels good to win.

MOM: Let's sit down and catch a breath.

KATE: Wait a minute, wait a minute! *(Music stops)* We're on the team, right, Susu? If the "boys" get to get on this team they have to agree to the rules.

GIRLS *line up, pull* MOM *with them.*

JAIMIE: What rules?

KATE: *(Kicking her)* You *know*: The rule that all money . . . if any, but we expect at least twenty-five thousand, if not a hundred million, but it could get up to that, if we sell our story to Walt Disney . . . all the money we take in from our work with our captured creature is to be shared equally. And each member has only one vote.

DAD: But you girls . . .

SUSU: *(All* GIRLS *take step forward, pulling* MOM *along)* Women!

DAD: You women outnumber us five to two.

DOUGIE: But Dad—they called us "boys·"

KATE: *(All women cross arms)* Right.

DAD: How do we know we can trust you?

KATE: You don't.

SUSU: You have to trust us as we have you.

DAD: Do you trust me? *(Silence)*

JAIMIE: *(Raises her hand)* I do.

KATE: I used to.

DAD: *(Kneels)* I want to be trusted.

KATE: *(Crosses to* DAD*)* I want to trust you—do you agree?

DOUGIE: But it's not equal, five against two.

KATE: *Grabs* DOUGIE's *collar, strangling him)* Look, pal, business is business. Are you on the team or not?

DAD: One vote is better than none, Dougie.

DOUGIE: But two men against five women?

MOM: *(Crosses to* DOUGIE*)* But Dougie—why do you make yourself think that way? Why, we're *seven human beings.*

DOUGIE: We are? Are we human beings and men too?

DAD: Yes, I guess we are. Count me in.

DOUGIE: *(Whines)* Well . . . O.K.

KATE: Doug, that's a wimpy answer.

DOUGIE: *(Reluctantly)* Yes . . . I'm on the team!

SUSU: Grab the camera, Mama!

MOM: *(Sings)* This outer turmoil cuts me like a knife.

SILVER MORGAN: Hark ark ark ark.

MOM: But you all look happy working.

SILVER MORGAN: Birk chirk.

MOM: Yes, you all look happy working.

SILVER MORGAN: Wolf wolf.

MOM: Is this the meaning of life?

SILVER MORGAN: Wuff wuff wuff.

ALL WOMEN: *(Sing and dance)* Eeeny meeny miney moe—

SILVER MORGAN: Hark ark.

WOMEN: Catch a pronoun by the toe.

SILVER MORGAN: Chirk irk.

WOMEN: If she hollers make her say—

SILVER MORGAN: Woof woof.

WOMEN: "I was born in the U.S.A."

SILVER MORGAN: Ruff muff.

WOMEN: Eeny meeny miney moe—

SILVER MORGAN: Chirk irk irk irk.

WOMEN: Catch a pronoun by the toe.

SILVER MORGAN: Hark ark ark ark.,

WOMEN: If she hollers make her say—

SILVER MORGAN: Woof woof.

WOMEN: "I was born in the U.S.A."

SILVER MORGAN: Ruff.

WOMEN: "U-S-A."

SILVER MORGAN: Muff.

WOMEN: "U-S-A."

JAIMIE: Hi yo Silver Morgan Connell!

JAIMIE: Do you think like you bark?

WHOLE FAMILY: Hi yo Silver Morgan Connell!

SILVER MORGAN: Or lurch like you church?

KATE: A new family member
With a name anyone can remember.

JAIMIE: Hi yo Silver!

DOUGIE: Hi yo Silver!

WHOLE FAMILY: Hi yo Silver Morgan Connell!

JAIMIE: I love you.

MOM: What a lark!

DAD: Do you think like you talk?

DOUGIE: Or talk like you think?

SILVER MORGAN: Bark ark, I luuuuuuv to
Bark ark, I uuuuuuufff to . . .
Hi yo Julie, it's me too!
Snap crackle popple,
Tower of Babble topple!

MOM: I love you.

KATE: A new family member
With a name anyone can remember.

SILVER MORGAN: I shirk yo too.

FAMILY: Hi yo Silver!

SILVER MORGAN: I grew through.

FAMILY: Hi yo Silver!

SILVER MORGAN: I good with you.

FAMILY: Hi yo Silver Morgan Connell!

SILVER MORGAN: I think you bark!

ALL: *(Entering cage with SILVER MORGAN)*
Eeny meeny miney moe,
Catch a pronoun by the toe.

SILVER MORGAN: *(To audience)* I bark you.

KATE: *(Bends bars of cage, jumps out, followed by SILVER MORGAN)*
If she barkers, let her think—

SILVER MORGAN: I was born in the kitchen sink. *(Crosses down-stage right with KATE)*

All except JAIMIE, who plays piano, sing and parade across stage in cage. KATE sings too but stays with SILVER MORGAN, who birks chirks and whistles to the song.

THE WHOLE FAMILY: *(Sings)* When is a human being,
Being a human being?
When is your mind dirty?
When are you called "purty"?
When do you sing like a lark?

SILVER MORGAN: Aaarrrrrk!

FAMILY: How do you know you're thinking when you bark—

SILVER MORGAN: Bark!

FAMILY: Bark—

SILVER MORGAN: Bark!

FAMILY: Bark?

SILVER MORGAN: Ark ark.

FAMILY: When is a human being—

SILVER MORGAN: Birrrrrrk!

FAMILY: Being a human being?
Do you bark like you think, or talk like you bark?

SILVER MORGAN: Bark!

FAMILY: Eat navy beans? Relish tree bark?

SILVER MORGAN: Wuuffff.

FAMILY: Do you think like you talk, or bark like you think?
Can you think like a lark?

SILVER MORGAN *and* KATE *cross to left and right of cage, push/pull it stage left nearer piano. All sing* out *to audience.*

FAMILY: It's a lark to sing,
It's a lark to sing.
It's a lark to sing!

SILVER MORGAN: Ark ark!

Lights fade out.

CURTAIN

Appendix: Teaching Aid

Here is a work sheet made out by playwright Megan Terry for use by the humanists, discussion leaders and teachers to aid in leading the audience and/or students in discussion after the presentation of the play.

Information to humanists working
with the Omaha Magic Theatre on
AMERICAN KING'S ENGLISH FOR QUEENS:

Language Processes At Work Within the Songs and Scenes

Prologue

Language of warm welcome and polite greeting. A reminder that animal sounds are a language too, and serve as a means of communication for animals as English does for us. Use of words some people find confusing these days: "humankind," "mankind," "womankind." First statement of the central question of the play: "Do you think like you talk or talk like you think?"

Act One, Scene One, *(Song: "You Speak English!")*

As they get ready for bed, the children play with sound and image juxtaposition, and wonder why they can't make up their own language. They know they can make up their own sounds, ask their parents what various sounds are called, and want to know why they can't name their sounds anything they want. The discovery that Dad's grandma was Spanish opens up more possibilities for playing with language, and the realization that English isn't the only "medium" through which the human mind can communicate with itself and others.

Act One, Scene Two, (Dad, Susu, *and the whole family*)

Dad gives a lesson in clear speech, which he believes helps you to be well-thought-of and helps propel you to a higher status in society. He wants his children to speak clearly and correctly and give them a better chance in life. Children use language of convenience and don't even hear its imperfections. They're frightened by not knowing what it is they're saying that's so "wrong," or what they've said to displease their father so. MOTHER helps dispel their fright by playing with the "incorrect" sounds with them as a nonsense chant.

ACT ONE, SCENE THREE *(Mother and young child)*

Confusion and "miss-communication" caused by the generic pronoun "he." This confusion, which makes some youngsters think all animals of certain species are male (e.g. dogs are boys and cats are girls), can carry over into adulthood.

ACT ONE, SCENE FOUR *(MOM in kitchen, children in family room)*

In the kitchen, the mother's own voice and words when she was 16 keep intruding on her consciousness as she works, interrupting her household duties and creating yearning, confusion and "inner turmoil." She tries to shut out the voice of her former self by throwing herself into making veal stew for the family. Meanwhile, the children are playing a girls' "career" game in the family room. Much of the language is taken from an actual commercial game for little girls. Its description of job roles and qualifications implies that only females do these jobs. Language shapes the youngsters' career expectations and their ideas of the qualities they need to have (or are allowed to show) if they're to suceed at certain jobs—even to how to stand, dress and put on makeup. The girls and the boy argue over what job roles are possible or appropriate, using lots of controlling and put-down language like: "You're too little," "too short," "too fat," "too emotional," "lazy," "crazy," "dopey." Male ballet dancers are characterized as "too short," stewardesses as mere "waitresses."

ACT ONE, SCENE FIVE *(SUSU, DAD, and MOM in kitchen)*

The language of young love and romance, via Top 40 music and fan magazines for today's teenagers, "golden oldie" standards for the over-30 set. The language of pop song lyrics has partly shaped their expectations, attitudes and behavior toward possible love partners. In MOM and DAD'S case it hypnotized them into romance and marriage and gave them conflicting expectations of life "ever after." The language of romance clashes with the language of money, as DAD tries to make MOM and teenage daughter face economic reality as he sees it.

ACT ONE, SCENE SIX (DAD *and* DOUGIE *in bathroom getting ready for church*)

This scene explores body language (especially "masculine" body language to win the respect of other males), the concepts of "tall" and "small," and what behavior is allowed if one is big or little, father or son. DAD uses example, threats, ridicule and his superior strength (all tactics that the playwright has observed in real life) to train his son to be a "man," saying, "Men don't cry—if you cry I'll make you wear your sister's clothes to school."

ACT TWO, SCENE ONE *(Snipe Hunt)*

The big kids against the little kids: "You're too little to know"/ "too little to do"/"too stupid." "You can't do this because you're sissies, girls and dinks." It's the language of "ageism" (older-kids-vs.-younger) and initiation, or put-down, power and barter.

ACT TWO, SCENE TWO (DAD *Meets the Snipe*)

The language of business from corporate economics to office skills, reveals how the males expect the females to dress and act at the office, and the threat to DAD's ego when his job is in danger, his secretary is taken away and he has to learn to type. The language of affluence—of "microwave," "mini-bikes," and "McDonald's"—brings out conflicting attitudes toward it in the family and toward the excessive use of energy which DAD is sure will turn them all into "marshmallows" who'll lose the ability to walk. The language of competition, as quoted by DAD says, "Quitters never win and winners never quit."

ACT TWO, SCENE THREE (DOUGIE *alone with the Snipe*)

Language of cruelty mixed with fantasy: "I can fly"/"You're locked up . . . (therefore) you're bad."

ACT TWO, SCENE FOUR *(Civilizing the Snipe)*

This final scene deals with winning another's confidence through body language and sound imitation; the language of teamwork; naming (and the use of names to control others' behavior); special emphasis on the pronoun "she." (The generic "he" is used so constantly in English that females have to live in a split world inside their heads, constantly translating and trying to reassure themselvs that they live here, too.) "Do you talk like you think or think like you talk?" (Does the fact that English is your "mother tongue" limit the range of your ability to think?) "When is a human being being a human being?"

OTHER OVER-ALL CONSIDERATIONS posed by the play as a whole include:

Music, dance and movement as languages of communication; the language of visual communication, covering everything from body language to sets and costumes; questions like, "Can you sing some things more easily than you can speak them?" The language of the text and subtext; multiple levels of imagery; the actors' facial expressions, tones of voice, gestures and attitudes as a language of communication over and above the text of the play.

Running Gag

Book and Structure by
Jo Ann Schmidman
Song Lyrics by Megan Terry
Music by Marianne de Pury
and Lynn Herrick

RUNNING GAG was first produced by the Omaha Magic Theatre in January of 1979. It was developed in workshops with the support of a grant from the Rockefeller Foundation. I wanted to take a closer look at America's then new fascination and preoccupation with running and jogging. So many contradictory reports—evidences that running was for everyone, warnings to female runners that your insides would drop out, running as meditation—emotional, psychological and physical reasons why or why not to run. I began running in the spring of 1978. It made me feel good. I continue to run at about 2:00 p.m. daily and for the rest of the day I feel totally revitalized as if I just woke up. I began to run as a warmup before performances—the run served to open me, my voice, and my body, allowing me to be more integrated with head and body. The Magic Theatre Company began running in November 1978—a brisk two-mile jog in whatever weather now precedes all regular physical and vocal workshops which precede all rehearsals at the Omaha Magic Theatre.

RUNNING GAG was presented in Omaha, Nebraska as a full production in January, 1979. With it the Omaha Magic Theatre has toured extensively in the Midwest and East. Perhaps the greatest honor to date was the invitation to perform RUNNING GAG at the 1980 Winter Olympics in Lake Placid, New York in February, 1980. We were one of two theatre companies invited by the National Fine Arts Committee to represent the United States at the 1980 activities. Response to RUNNING GAG from international athletes and Olympic audiences was one of enthusiastic support and surprise that such important work was begin done in Omaha, Nebraska. I remember skiers from Sweden after an Olympic presentation coming forward to embrace Omaha Magic Theatre company members not only as artists, but as fellow athletes. RUNNING GAG is still in the Omaha Magic Theatre's touring repertoire.

The Omaha Magic Theatre's production of RUNNING GAG was directed and structured by Jo Ann Schmidman with soft-sculpture design by Diane Degan and Megan Terry. Soft-sculpture execution was by Elizabeth Scheuerlein. Lyrics are by Megan Terry with music by Marianne de Pury and Lynn Herrick and musical structure by Marianne de Pury.

I would like to thank the Rockefeller Foundation, the National Endowment for the Arts, the Ford Foundation, Mark Ross and Olympic National Fine Arts Committee, the city of Omaha, and the CETA program for support in the realization of this work.

RUNNING GAG has turned out to be the biggest success and longest running play in the Omaha Magic Theatre's ten-year history.

Happy Running

Jo Ann Schmidman

The Place: A marathon along the Missouri River. The marathon of a young woman running toward self realization and her womanhood. The marathon of one's interior (head) running sometimes with/sometimes without one's exterior (body). A race of the subjective (who you feel you are) with the objective (who others think you are) toward the essential (who you really are).

The Setting: RUNNING GAG may be performed on a standard indoor or outdoor proscenium. A director may choose to stage it in an open space, in the round, thrust, or as part of a real marathon run. The Omaha Magic Theatre, in touring situations has performed it in every possible way and it worked as theatre every time.

The Costumes: The actors wear uniform colorful jogging shorts, T-shirts or tank tops and running shoes. Soft-sculpture pieces helping to define individual charcter are velcroed onto the running garb. (Velcro is to allow easy and frequent washing.) SPOKESPERSON wears golden soft-sculptured wings on the arms on her T-shirt; LOVER, a giant soft-sculpture everlast muscle belt and a hairy chest made of pulled yarn; HUSBAND, soft-sculpture satin lapels and bow tie; MOTHER carries a soft-sculpture ditty bag and wears soft-sculpture furs and jewels; FRIEND wears a large soft-sculpture alligator over the pocket of her (latest in sportswear) shirt. Other runners may wear soft-sculpture bandaids over a bleeding nipple, may carry an extra pair of soft-sculpture shoes, may carry a soft-sculpture brown-bag lunch, may wear a soft-sculpture banner or top hat . . .

The actors (all except RUNNER), instead of wearing the usual entry number worn by all marathoners, wear 4" x 6" soft-sculpture labels hand-embroidered by each actor with his or her character name, e.g., HUSBAND, MOTHER, . . . The other runners may select a number which they embroider on a similar label.

The Musical Structure: Running is a kinetic musical act. The feet beat a rhythm into the earth, the heart beats a counter-rhythm within the breath, and arms regularly push at the air without. Silence within constant percussive drumming is essential to the run. Environmental sounds, as characters of the run, jam with the figure of RUNNER as she maintains her constant rhythm. These sounds act as distractions (the villain obstacle) of the run and as propellants (supporting cast) carrying the runner effortlessly forward. Marianne de Pury worked with Ms. Schmidman from the first RUNNING GAG workshop in order to fully explore the essential sound structure of the run.

CHARACTERS

RUNNER
SPOKESPERSON FOR INDUSTRY
HUSBAND
LOVER
MOTHER
FRIEND
*Other Runners in the Marathon

SOFT-SCULPTURE CHARACTERS

DOLLY PARTON
SUPERMAN
BEANIED BLONDE RUNNER
CRYING CLOUD
TREES

*Because of the nature of the piece, the number of runners may be greater or fewer depending on how many actors are available. At the Omaha Magic Theatre, young actors wishing to become a part of the theatre ensemble immediately began performing in this piece as 'other runners'. These non-speaking runner roles are on stage throughout the play. RUNNING GAG may be used as a training exercise to maintain focus, transformation of character, and physical control and endurance for the actor.

Musical Numbers

"INTENSITY" (Runner)
music by Marianne de Pury

"THE CURE FOR CANCER" (Friend)
music by Lynn Herrick

"WHY DO YOU RUN?"
(Runner and Chorus)
music by Lynn Herrick

"BLAH TO RUNNING" (Spokesperson)
music by Marianne de Pury

"WHAT DO YOU DO?" (Friend and Chorus)
music by Marianne de Pury

"I KNOW I'M GOIN'"
(Runner, Friend and Spokesperson)
music by Lynn Herrick

Lights preset, representing early dawn. Playing area prosceniuim, 20' wide, 30' deep. At the Omaha Magic Theatre, we performed on a 3' X 4' X 12' platform and a 10' X 5' ramp leading up to it. This entire area was covered in black astroturf.

There are six speaking parts in the play, but as many actors as make up the company may participate in the piece as runnners. Initially, at the Omaha Magic Theatre, we had only six performers, but as the company expanded with apprentices and new workshop participants, RUNNING GAG *was used as a training tool to explore image works, focus, and the ultimate acting exercise of integration of one's mind with one's body. It is important to note that the physical images suggested in the stage directions must be worked out in workshop/rehearsal sessions prior to the performance.*

The actors enter. House lights remain on. To warm up, they jog around the playing area. At the Omaha Magic Theatre our theatre was such that the actors could run in a serpentine pattern from the playing area to the lobby, back and forth. They assemble after several laps in the playing area. They prepare for the run: some re-tie shoe laces, work out tight muscles, practice sprint starts, others keep warm by doing stretches while waiting for the starting pistol. This time should be used by the actors to connect with, i.e., really look at, the audience—acknowledge friends—in order to relax into the sport. (Especially important for near-sighted performers, this prestart was done with eyeglasses. When the play starts they may remove the glasses or use sport glasses.)

RUNNER *runs non-stop throughout the seventy minutes of the piece. The other actors, when in scenes with* RUNNER, *or when involved in running images, must also keep up the run. The run may transform, become a run of a part of the body, i.e., a run on hands and knees , or a torso run. It is essential that every* movement *which involves covering distance during the play be a "run."*

The house lights black out. The actors form a pack in the dark. Silently, they set sights on their goals. A bull or ram's horn is sounded. The actors run in place. The audience should be allowed to experience this first run for several beats as pure audio in the blackout, focusing on the sound of the individual rhythms of each runner's run. The lights slowly *come* up *on this pack. The actors continue to run in place as a pack.*

The Push Run*: (An important repeated image in the piece) The actors remain in a pack, but begin to move across the space physically connected to one another. They vie for a prime position, try to be first, try to break out of the group. While vying, the actors remain focused on their goals: winning, surviving, or the finish line (if it is 26 miles away, they imagine it). Winning is very important to each of these runners. Each, throughout the* push run, *experiences triumph at being first or stongest or fastest or feeling good, as well as feeling fear at losing a position, or disappointment as others move up and take over. At the Omaha Magic Theatre, the actors had to contain this run in a three-foot-square area. During the* push run, *the actors individully continue to explore changes. in run-rhythm.*

RUNNER *begins in the pack as part of the* push run. *The pack moves within the three-foot area, vying for position from Stage Right to Stage Left.* RUNNER *is separated from other competetive group. She willfully continues (unconcerned with her loss of position; she is running for herself) exploring varied run-rhythms. Downstage Right, the pack continues to vie, then moves as a group backwards up the ramp. Then, still on the ramp, they move as a group Upstage Right.*

This first image sets the tone for the piece. It must not be rushed. As the pack moves far right, one actor transforms into the animal part of her/himself. At this sharp change, all the actors in the pack transform. RUNNER *keeps running Down Right. Previous workshop time must be spent exploring the animal part of each actor—how this image is physicalized, how this creature-part of oneself breathes, how it runs. The actors run as their animal selves through the space. They are being pursued—the run is a survival run. Each actor must fill out his own story—why and by whom (s)he is being chased.*

One by one, the actors, as creatures, gather Center on and around the ramp. Alert, they watch and listen. Their attention now changes to being intent on getting their dinner. Out of this image of animal selves stalking their prey, a "breath jam" insues. This jam is the same as that used by jazz musicians when they improvise with one another.

*For this "breath jam" the actors must listen carefully to one another
(as they listen for their prey). Individual breath stops and starts within
the jam. The sound of the breath rises and falls. Each creature breath
should correspond to this stalk / hunt. During this, RUNNER continues
her run, exploring her animal breathing and sensitivities. This image
is about breath rhythm and the game of survival. The actors smell or
hear an imagined prey approach. One actor conducts a stop of their
breathing. Each then lunge for their individual prey. One actor
(designated as conductor) breaks from this attack. All follow this
example and begin again the creature breath jam. Again each lunges
in unison for their prey. RUNNER gives several fully resonant wolf
howls. The actors transform into human beings chasing or being
chased. During preparatory workshop it is advisable that each actor
finds separate and distinct runs to show clearly who is running, where
(s)he's running, and why (s)he's running. Each of these runs must
have to do with survival. (The stronger the life/death situation that
the actor chooses, the clearer the image will be, e.g., stalking a frog
for dinner or being chased by a lion.) Each actor in her/his own time,
transforms from Run 1 to Run 2 to Run 3. Each actor chooses a
floor pattern to be covered for each of the three runs, e.g., a circle
around the entire space, a verticle line back to front, a horizontal line
twice covered, a jagged irregular shape across the floor . . . the pattern
possibilities are infinite.*

*As each actor completes the floor pattern of the third run, each
continues this third run in place. This will serve to magically unify
the actors. All in their own time will sense the lack of movement across
the floor and begin their run in place.*

*The next image is run 3 performed as a torso run. (A torso run is a
run from the waist up. The feet never leave the floor.) The torso run
is done in unison to a count of five. The next image the actors work
with is a runner's personal fear. Each works with a personal image
and a fearful breath rhythm, also done to a count of five. The torso
run continues through the physical image of what the runner fears.
The ensemble moves with fearful breath up the ramp to form a line
on the upper platform. A woodblock is hit. The actors turn together
in response to the sound. They look to the right. The woodblock is hit
again. The actors turn in unison and look left. RUNNER continues to
run. Each actor specifically identifies the woodblock sound. The
response of each actor is determined by what (s)he imagines the sound
to be, i.e., a twig, a bear, a snake, a gunshot.*

Two actors release themselves from the pull of the sound in the brush, the woods, (or however each has justified the pull) To look first right, then left. They then slowly jog down the ramp, conferring sotto voce *as they jog.* RUNNER, *continuing to run, crosses Stage Left. With the seriousness of a summit meeting the two plan how to play a game of "leap frog." Then they play—first one leaps, then the other. The other actors, still looking left on the upper platform, respond each time the Downstage actors' feet hit the floor, just as they responded to the woodblock sound. This game is to support running/jogging as adult play.*

One of the actors on the platform makes the piercing sound of a falcon or another bird of prey. RUNNER *is pulled Center by this sound. The two leapfrog actors are pulled back onto the platform as if drawn by the cry. The other actors are pulled up and out of themselves by the sound. All respond to the image in the sky. Now all the actors except* RUNNER *are brought together on the upper platform. They crouch, determined, a starting line about to take off for a sprint. They* strain *with the* anxiety *of the short race, knowing the takeoff is most important. The actors feel each other's held-back energy. When the tension builds to its highest pitch, they take off simultaneously. It is a flop—some fall on their faces, somersault, flip—one does not move but pretends (s)he has.* RUNNER *continues to run Downstage Center. The actors curl over their knees and massage their lower backs.*

In the following speech/prayer, each time "running" is said, an actor pops up to her/his knees and torso runs leading with some part of the body—top of the head/head hanging, chin, chest, arm, shoulder, etc. they run this way throughout the prayer. This torso run, with one part of the body leading, gives us a look at how different individuals run.

RUNNER: *(Joyfully runs and prays)*
Dearest God,
    You are perfect
    I am in your arms
Dearest God,
    My life is yours,
    You are perfect.
Dearest God
    I am running for your life; (HUSBAND *pops up*)
Your life is eternal, dearest God.

You designed us for running. (MOTHER *pops up*)
I am fulfilling your design,
    Running (SPOKESPERSON *pops up*)
    to you,
for you,
full of you.

The human body is designed for running. (FRIEND and LOVER
pop up)
Forgive me
    for the first thirty years;
I sat in apple pie
        order
stuffing
    my head.

Now the stuffing's out of date,
But I know it's not too late
    because
I'm running (*Full of self, knees are lifted higher and higher*)
    I'm running.
And I'm running
    to keep on—
running.

RUNNER *performs a joyous breath chant to the rhythm of her run.
The other actors continue to lead with selected parts of their bodies.
At final "running" of* RUNNER'S *prayer the actors remain on knees
(count of five), rise (count of five), torso run in standing position
(count of five), and run in place lifting feet. After this final five
count, the actors run and join in the breath jam with the* RUNNER.

*One of the actors sounds a ratchet (city noise). The actors all crunch
together in the center of upper platform. The actors huddle close for
safety in numbers, warmth, security, to survive life in the city. The
ratchet sounds again. They move Stage Right: ratchet sounds, they
move Stage Left. Other piercing, shattering sounds of the city (cymbals,
horns, bells), the actors turn to the right and run. During this run,
the actors explore images of some of the relationships of runners during
a marathon run, e.g., waving to a pal, running with a spouse, helping
a cramped fellow, competing, playing, hurting, etc. They pass a soft
sculpture-covered spray-bottle of water amongst them.*

SPOKESPERSON FOR INDUSTRY *sees* RUNNER *running Downstage, separates her/himself from the others and catches up with her. They run side by side,* RUNNER *pulling ahead now and again in profile toward Stage Right.*

SPOKESPERSON: (*Hoping* RUNNER *is potential buyer*) Hi. These new "Pony" shoes are the best I've ever worn.

RUNNER: (*Looks at* SPOKESPERSON *and changes direction, runs in place facing the audience*)

SPOKESPERSON: Jim Bush, head track and field coach at UCLA says . . .

RUNNER: Hi, Jim. (*Pulls ahead*)

SPOKESPERSON: I'm not Jim, I'm Bob.

RUNNER: Bye, Bob. (*Changes direction*)

SPOKESPERSON: Where'd you get your shoes?

RUNNER: At Tarjay. ("*Target*"—*a local discount store—said with a French accent*)

SPOKESPERSON: (*Disgusted, doubles over, gags, pivots in a circle. This is yet another selling device*) Ughhh. (*then a quick change to con her*) Do you hate your feet?

RUNNER: They were on sale.

SPOKESPERSON: They're the only feet you'll ever have. These "Pony" shoes I'm wearing have been run-tested. Track and field athletes at UCLA swear by them. These're the most advanced running shoes on the market today. Anatomically and bio-mechanically developed and *scientifically* tested.

RUNNER: (*Silence, running and breathing*)

SPOKESPERSON: (*Stops, "hard sell"*) Do you want to be a member of the "now" generation?

RUNNER: (*Smiles and bounces belly-to-belly playfully into* SPOKESPERSON, *then runs Front.* SPOKESPERSON *is surprised, but turns Front and catches up to her again*)

SPOKESPERSON: The heart of these great new shoes is their sole. (*Crash on cymbal*) Want to try them on?

RUNNER: Later, I'm busy.

SPOKESPERSON: (*To audience*) The "Pony" VSD sole, (*aside*) patent pending, (RUNNER *slows down, drops back to the ramp, changes direction*) insures optimal shock absorption, pronation and forward motion at the ball of the foot. This is achieved through specially designed nipples on . . .

RUNNER: (*To the other runners*) Did you ever feel such fresh air? (*She takes a deep breath. All the actors,* SPOKESPERSON *too, turn Front, inhale audibly*)

SPOKESPERSON *takes positive credit for a successful first sales approach. Transforms to "hero" crossing the finish line" image. Runs in a circle with finish line image, then joins others on platform.*

Image: Demonstrating breathing. At the Omaha Magic Theatre air was taken in the nose, out the mouth—in the mouth, out the nose—in the nose . . . RUNNER *runs Downstage Center. Her run rhythm changes. We can tell she is about to share some serious thoughts.*

RUNNER: I want you to know the natural order of things.
I don't want you wondering about me
while you sit and watch and think.
I'll tell you right now I'm an Aries!
I'm doing things.
I'm doing things to my body.
I believe in my body.
I believe that you can make your body work for you.
Mine will.
I believe in the will.

The actors run onto the playing area. They each stop at her/his own time and demonstrate a personal will, e.g., attempting to stop smoking, willing oneself to look thin by sucking in one's cheeks in a mirror, enduring enormous pain, resisting specific lust, etc. When the action becomes too intense to willfully resist, the actor runs away to a new space, and demonstrates another personal will. This continues throughout the speech. At the Omaha Magic Theatre, two actors exert their wills through giant soft sculpture images of Dolly Parton and Superman which they carry. Dolly and Superman kiss and tease each other as an allurement to RUNNER. RUNNER *willfully decides not to join them, but to continue her run.*

RUNNER: If you know anything about Aries—the Aries whose
birthdays are nearer Taurus than Pisces—then you will under-
stand I have a will—an enormous will.
  My birthday is one day from Hitler's.
  I'm only now beginning to appreciate my will.
  My will has always been far larger to people
who've had to deal with me than it has been to me.
  My will is big.
(*Quietly*) I think my will is bigger than my body.
I've been learning to use my will.
Why should others be in awe of my will and me
not get any good out of it?
  Since I have it,
  I've decided to love it
and train it.
Mark that, (*Excited breath*)
it's the key.
(*Increases running rhythm to match breath*)
I've been doing quite well in the training
of my will.
  You want to know how strong I'm getting my will?
  I've got it so strong
  that you could bring in the grandest feast,
right in here
right now
(*Actor should substitute her own town's best restaurants*)
  from the French Cafe, or V. Mertz or the Old Vienna,
  or the best meal your or my mother
ever cooked . . .
  bring it in here! And I will show you my will,
  I will sit down with you
  and watch you eat it,
  but I won't take a bite.
  Not one bite.
  I don't have to eat if I don't will it.
  I can *not* eat.
  I can *not* eat for days.
  I love chocolate.
  I won't eat it.
  I won't even eat hot chocolate chip cookies
fresh from my oven.

(Turns, strut runs in profile)
    I love clothes.
    I have a Leo moon, and a thin body. Clothes
look fabulous on me.
    My mother cries with happiness when she takes
me shopping
        because anything I put on looks great.
        (Teasing) You want to know how strong I am?
        (Explosively runs front)
        You can bring in racks of clothes.
        (Actor may substitute local clothing stores)
        You can bring in the latest fashions
        from Brandeis, Plaza Suite, Zoob's.
        You can import from Sak's Fifth Avenue, or
Filene's in Boston.
        You can send to Paris for clothes from St. Laurent.

    I won't put them on.
    I won't wear them anywhere.
    I won't even buy at sales.
    Not even at 50 percent mark-off sales.
    (Jazzy introduction to song: "Intensity" begins)
    The "Good Will" is enough to dress my will.

As music begins, the actors strike images of hanging out, very laid back, on street corners. They keep time to the music while in the condition of "nodding off."

RUNNER: *Sings*
Very intensely
Flexes muscles   Yeah, health is o.k.
Bumps   And fitness fine,
                          But I like to be
All are thrown against up against the wall
wall by imagined force all the time.

(ALL: *heads right*)   I'm an intensity junkie,
ALL: *heads left*   I'm an intensity child,
ALL: *heads front*   I'm an intensity freak,
                          I can't stand quiet and mild,
All do wild and   I'm wild!
crazy gestures.

All dangle from waist	I want to live
	at top pitch,
All reach up	Blessedness is in the reach
All fall	There's no time to be rich.
Ensemble images	
of intensity	Intensity,
	Intensity,
	Intensity
	Is my divinity!
	Intensity,
	Intensity,
	Intensity
	is my divinity!
During music actors	
crawling seductively	
up ramp	
	If I haven't just fallen in love,
All balance on a	I'll walk on a ledge
high-rise ledge	Without a net
Fall	Above the crowd
Hard torso run on knees	I'll do anything on a bet;
Flat on bellies	Sleep is a waste,
Eyes wide open,	If I'm not delirious, I'm not awake!
Flip to backs	
Seductive isolations	I'm in love, I'm in love,
with one part of body	I'm in love, I'm in love,
e.g., shoulder,	I'm in love with love and romance!
chest, leg . . .	
	I'm in love, I'm in love,
	I'm in love, I'm in love,
	I'm in love with love and romance!
Pairs of actors, nose	
to nose. A large step	
with arm swing is taken	
on each beat of song.	
One of each pair moves	
back as other moves	I can't stand quiet,
forward	I'm an earthquake,
Jump forward	Don't talk to me about eternal peace,
	I love it here in edge city!

All perform images of intensity	Intensity, Intensity, Intensity Is my divinity!
	Intensity, Intensity, Intensity Is my divinity!
	Intensity– – Is my divinity!

The actors, exhausted, jog from side to side across the playing area. In unison, they mumble and repeat complaints under their breath.

HUSBAND: I eat too much . . .

SPOKESPERSON: I wish I was ten pounds lighter . . .

LOVER: I wish clothes looked good on me . . .

MOTHER: I wish I didn't huff and puff when I walk up two flights of stairs . . .

FRIEND: I wish I could live to be ninety and enjoy my own mind . . .

The mumbling/complaining is established. This becomes a quiet "I wish" chorus jam under RUNNER'S *next speech.*

RUNNER: (*To the audience, tries to be tactful*) I don't want you to take this personally. What I'm going to say next is possibly what you—
many of you—
have said to yourselves over and over . . .

Each actor in turn takes their above line to the audience, then continues side-to-side jog while mumbling and complaining.

RUNNER: (*Simultaneously to the company's complaints*) 'I eat too much' or 'I wish I was ten pounds lighter' or 'I wish clothes looked good on me' (*mockingly grabs heart*) or 'I wish I didn't huff and puff when I walk up two flights of stairs' or (*meekly*) 'I wish I could live to be ninety and enjoy my own mind.'

As this builds, actors change from "beating up" on themselves to "asking for someone's help."

RUNNER: 'I wish, I wish, I wish' or (*Cynically*) 'I'll try.'

All flip over on their backs like flailing beetles. They run as if the floor were above them.

RUNNER: That's the trouble with Americans lately. They've turned into (*wistfully*) "I wish I'll try," or (*wistfully*) "I'll even try to wish" . . . (*jog while boxing*) instead of what we used to be—the great nation of can-doers!
　During and after World War II
　We showed 'em, we showed 'em, we showed the world
　we could do anything.
　We even helped our enemies make their countries
into the Garden of Eden.
　Now don't take this personally, but most Americans have duck's disease. (*Turns and slaps her ass two whacks, and waddles*)

*The actors, insulted, get up and exit. New image—*MOTHER *and* LOVER *come together and move to the platform. They "show" themselves in unison, like police mug shots: Face front, profile, profile, face front, face front, other side profile. They keep repeating these.*

RUNNER: Because of hard work resulting in prosperity, we are now able to feed the rest of the world.
　(*in confidence*) But *we* eat too much at our own tables before we ship the bread overseas.
　I know this is not news to you,
　it's as familiar as the "Three Bears." But you know, and *I* know the "Three Bears" have gotten fat and lazy and "Goldilocks" can steal them blind and run circles around them and all the "Three Bears" do is lay in their beds, out of breath, and say (*in papa bear's voice*), "I wish I had more energy. I wish I could get my 'getup and go' to come back and get me." (MOTHER *and* LOVER *exit*)
　YOU can do it! You can do it,
　if you do what I've done, and start right now to train your will.

FRIEND: (*Runs in*) How ya doing?

RUNNER: My husband just informed me I have to learn finance.

FRIEND: What's what?

RUNNER: That's what I asked.

FRIEND: Doesn't he know about it?

RUNNER: I think so. He did once, but now seems uncertain.

FRIEND: If he knows about it, why do you have to?

RUNNER: In case something happens to him.

FRIEND: He's so young. (*Music begins*)

SPOKESPERSON: (*Runs by*) My mother says the locusts are coming.

RUNNER: They can eat the grasshoppers.

FRIEND: (FRIEND *and* SPOKESPERSON *dance/run together*) Eat, drink, and be merry. We'll all be broke in five years.

RUNNER: (*Taken back*) Five?

Music builds, then stops abruptly. The actors stop, dance/run, jump front, and begin backward up ramp with "Sisyphus" image. Finish line gets nearer and nearer. When each almost crosses it, it moves further away. This image repeats through entire next scene.

After they back up the ramp, they form a line on the platform. HUSBAND *soon gets a pain from over-exertion, (He is out of shape) he doubles over from it, but soon regains his cool and continues to run. Another pain stops him. He sees* RUNNER *and attempts to catch up. He is crippled with another pain but covers it up. He continues to run for the sake of his self-image.* RUNNER *runs in profile toward the right.*

HUSBAND: (*Runs up behind her*) Drink this. (*Offers her a soft sculpture-covered plant sprayer containing water*)

RUNNER *takes water into her mouth, gurgles, mimes spitting it back out and pours it over her head. returns sprayer to* HUSBAND.

HUSBAND: Good?

RUNNER: Great.

HUSBAND: (*Takes her around, leans on her*) It's going to be a leaner Hanukkah-Christmas than we thought. (*She turns in his arms to face him*)

RUNNER: (*Belly to belly run*) *I'm* going to be leaner.

HUSBAND: Sure you are, our profits were just wiped out.

RUNNER: What profits?

HUSBAND: (*He sinks to the floor*) The market dropped a hundred points.

RUNNER: (*Turns her back to him and kicks up her heels which seem to hit* HUSBAND. *He protects himself*) I don't care.

HUSBAND: You've got to learn about it.

RUNNER: Why?

HUSBAND: (*Rises*) In case something happens to me.

RUNNER: When we got married (*Slow version of the "Wedding March" begins*) you promised to take care of everything that had to do with numbers

HUSBAND: (*Sees finish line. Torso run, revs self up*) My brother-in-law died at thirty-six. (*Runs into a wall, falls, Wedding March ends abruptly*)

RUNNER: (*Picking him up*) You promised we're both living to eighty-five and then we're both going together.

HUSBAND: (*Sees finish line. Torso run, revs self up*) I know, but you can never tell. (*Runs into wall, a loud crack, he falls*)

RUNNER: (*Turns and runs away*) I have enough to do.

HUSBAND: (*Urgently gets up, tries to catch up with her. Very fast exchange*) You have to learn, I can't do it alone anymore. Unprecedented things are happening. (*They run very fast. Image:* RUNNER'S *back pressed to* HUSBAND'S *front—in place, running very fast*)

RUNNER: You've always told me not to judge the present by the past.

HUSBAND: Do as I say and not as I do. I'm afraid of a margin-call.

RUNNER: You'll get a chance to make it back. "Wall Street always gives you a second chance."

HUSBAND: Wall Street will, but West Germany might not. (*To exit, he turns around, back to audience. They run back to back and pivot in a circle*)

RUNNER: (*As she pivots to face front, confused, as an aside to herself and audience*) I thought we won the war.

HUSBAND: (*As he pivots to face front, calling to* RUNNER) Don't trust anyone *over* . . . seas! (*He runs off.* RUNNER, *puzzled, pivots to front and moves down left*)

HUSBAND *runs to base of ramp. The others run in to form "V" of birds. Image: Ducks flying south formation. They begin to jam with light "Da Da Da Da Da" sounds. Each with her/his own enjoyment of the run.* MOTHER *begins to groan. There may be a psychological or physical reason for this. The other actors (including* RUNNER*) must try not to be seduced by the sounds of the groaner into feeling their own pain. We see them resist the pull of pain, sometimes they are pulled into the sympathetic slow-groan rhythm. Ultimately, out of frustration with the push-pull of the opposition, the actors move in an irregular circular movement. "Da Da" jam continues.* SPOKESPERSON *and* LOVER *join forces, remove themselves from the group, and run downstage with strong "Da Da's". The others, except* MOTHER *and* HUSBAND*, join.* RUNNER'S *rhythm is slowed. She is pulled closer to her mother up the ramp.* HUSBAND *gets a stitch, he groans, but manages to join the others Downstage. The other actors maintain, visibly ignore* HUSBAND*, and run further away from his pain, Stage Right.*

The actors change to slow motion torso runs, focusing on how the body moves as each changes her/his center of gravity to different parts of the body. Image of willow trees running with the wind.

RUNNER: (*From platform up right, running with* MOTHER) Maybe I should have stuck with swimming?
   If seventy-one-year-old Walter Stack can run eight marathons a year, I can too.
   He didn't give up swimming.
   (*Drooping*) If there was just more time in a day
   I could keep swimming, too. I love swimming.
   My dog always went swimming with me in my mother's swimming pool,
      but she sold it.

But out here—out of the water,
I got the trees and the grass
(*Feels wetness of hair and face*)
and with all the sweat—it's water! My own water!
And all the toxins are swimming out of my system—
that's got to make me feel great.
I do feel great.
I'll just run past the pain.
Just keep running past the pain.
The pain is only pain.
The pain is only physical.
(*Slowly more decisive torso run*)
I can get behind the pain. It goes away when I dream.

The actors continue slowly examining center-of-gravity runs as they back to their new positions. For next image, MOTHER *picks up soft sculpture of crying cloud. For this image, the actors on hands and knees explore different images of flowing, rippling, and running water. (They are* RUNNER'S *trail of tears) This continues throughout the next scene.*

RUNNER: I'd rather have this (*Holds side*) pain in my side
than all the pains I've had in my head.
  Mental pain is heavy.
  Mental pain is heaviest.
  Physical pain blots out mental pain. It's easier to
deal with.
  (*Runs down ramp, down Stage Right*)
  Agony, I embrace you. Agony, I embrace you because
I feel you.
  One has perspective on physical pain—
  It's a thing.
  Mental pain is all pervasive and beats down on one
from above.
  Mental pain sits on my brain
  a foot kicking each eyeball.

MOTHER *moves the cloud in a movement jam with* RUNNER'S *words: "Agony, I embrace you."* HUSBAND *is down center,* LOVER *is on the ramp,* SPOKESPERSON *is on the platform. They form a trail of tears.*

In the next scene, RUNNER *speaks flatly, with no tone in her voice.*

FRIEND: (*In water image, in her hands and knees on platform up right*) Why are you crying?

RUNNER: Am I?

FRIEND: That's how I found you.

RUNNER: What?

FRIEND: You've left a trail of tears.

RUNNER: Me?

FRIEND: (*Gets up, skips over/splashes through by running over* LOVER *and* HUSBAND) I'm your friend, I'd know your tears anywhere.

RUNNER: I'm crying.

FRIEND: (*Touching* RUNNER) You rarely cry. It makes me cry to see you cry.

RUNNER: (*Uncertain, pulls way*) Why?

FRIEND: (*Excited, runs stage right*) Maybe it's like yawning?

RUNNER: Maybe it is. I haven't heard that it was.

FRIEND: Still excited, runs to RUNNER) Should we report it?

RUNNER: Where?

FRIEND: (*To audience, smiling, triumphant*) To science! (*Very fast run rhythm change. She runs backward up ramp.* RUNNER *runs in place a fast triumphant run.*)

All rise and join this triumphant, speedy run backward up ramp. LOVER *and* HUSBAND *run up on either side of* FRIEND, *pick her up, she runs in mid-air.* LOVER *and* HUSBAND *put* FRIEND *down, all stop in unison and time their pulses. They each look at watches, touch place where their pulse is strongest—temple, groin, neck, wrist, each arm—then look out as the count pulse beats.*

RUNNER *joyfully continues fast "science run." The actors count pulse to twenty.* LOVER *breaks the image and all run to a new space.* HUSBAND *runs to center of ramp and reclines to take pulse/all stop simultaneously.* HUSBAND *counts beats of his groin, sitting on ramp.*

HUSBAND: (*Looks up, notices* RUNNER *running her heart out*) If you want to work so hard, I wish you'd take up coal mining.

RUNNER: This isn't work.

HUSBAND: The sweat's rolling off you.

RUNNER: My friend said it was tears.

HUSBAND: *(Rises, runs up to her)* You cry! Hah! Hah! *(Mock/laugh at her)* Hah, hah . . .

RUNNER: I never cry.

HUSBAND: *(Massaging her shoulders)* Do you realize that coal miners stand to earn $35,000 a year in the best mines in Appalachia?

RUNNER: That's great.

HUSBAND: *(Sends her off with a knee to her bottom)* Here's a bus ticket.

RUNNER: I have my job.

HUSBAND: I just thought since you want to get all your muscles in shape you could be bringing home the bread, too.

RUNNER: Hey, it's the sun.
Hey, it's the trees.
Hey, it's the air.
Hey it's being able to move *(She runs into him. This image repeats through* HUSBAND'S *next line.)* without running into a stone wall.

HUSBAND: We have to pay twelve percent on our mortgage. I wish you'd get your head out of the clouds.

RUNNER: *(Runs hard in place)* My feet are on the ground.

HUSBAND: *(Listens to the vibrations of the running on the earth, his ear to the ground. Lifts head, an aside to audience.)* That's what you think. *(He returns to the ground to listen.)*

Duck call is sounded.

During the next scene, HUSBAND *moves to several places on the ramp to listen for running, ear to the ground.*

MOTHER *and* SPOKESPERSON, FRIEND *and* LOVER *perform image of child's first walk. (At Omaha Magic Theatre, we referred to this image as the bear dance.) One actor places her/his feet on top of her/his partner's. They both shift their weight from side to side and in this way walk.*

RUNNER: *(Calling to* FRIEND, *who is engaged in first walk image, down left)* I'm not racing, I just want to keep moving. *(To audience)* Passing thirty woke me up. I was in that band at Boston University. We took over the administration building, we chanted "Don't trust anyone over thirty!" I'm not racing, I just don't want to slow down.

FRIEND *and* LOVER *pick up heart-soft-sculpture-quilt and behind it move across playing area up the ramp. As the heart moves to where he is listening,* HUSBAND *joins them. They move to up right on platform. One of the actors hits against the quilt from behind to give the appearance of the heart beating.*

RUNNER: Every time I walk downtown to *(substitute local popular department store)* Brandeis, to shop with the blue-haired ladies, I'm reminded of how a body can just ruuuuunnn-down. *(With new hope)* I hope I've started early enough to train myself. Training myself. I thought I'd be trained by eighteen. Then I thought I'd be trained by the time I got my degree, but my twenties were just the beginning of my training. While I was training my head, my body got rusty. What if an atomic war comes, who will get the family into the Canadian Rockies to safety? One of us must be able to endure. *(Flinging one arm, then the other arm over her back representing the great weight of children on her back, she bends and runs under this weight.)* Could I carry my children on my back like the Chinese women in the long march? Not yet.

FRIEND, HUSBAND, MOTHER *run out from behind heart (*LOVER *behind heart continues to hold it), down the ramp and circle back up ramp where they lie feet up, heads toward the bottom of the ramp.*

RUNNER: *(Lowers her head and concentrates on endurance as she carries her children)* Not yet.

Musical introduction to "The Cure for Cancer" begins. LOVER *walks slowly with the heart to center of platform.*

LOVER: *(Peeks out over top of quilt and sings)* I have the answer. *(Hides behind quilt)*

HUSBAND, MOTHER, FRIEND: *(Reach toward* LOVER, *sigh and idolize him as if he were the athlete savior)* Ahhhhhh.

LOVER: *(Peeks around side of heart and teasing, sings)* The cure for cancer.

HUSBAND, MOTHER, FRIEND: *(Sigh and idolize him as before)* Ahhhhhh.

LOVER: *(Rubs against heart as if it were a big bath towel and sings)* Ohhhhhh, *(Seductive pose)* Don't work. *(Another seductive pose)* Don't eat. *(Bumps while pumping heart in and out behind head)* Don't breathe the air from the sky above. *(Seductively sneaking up on others on ramp)* The only thing still healthy to do— *(*LOVER *spreads heart quilt over the other actors)* Stay under the covers and make, make love.

A percussion solo. RUNNER *is miraculously freed from the weight on her shoulders. She begins a hot and heavy run, "making love" to the audience as she runs.* LOVER *builds to the point of joining others who are "making love" under quilt. They carry on under the heart throughout the percussion riff. A leg pops out. An arm, a head emerges to catch a fresh breath.* LOVER *crawls out, clearly beaten. He runs back and forth on top of platform—his version of a cold shower. He stops center, winded. His paranoia is evident again. He looks over his shoulder, right, runs in place, looks at his shoulder, left, and runs. He ducks, then looks up and pulls the quilt from the others and covers himself with it.*

When quilt is removed, exposing them, MOTHER *and* HUSBAND *run down right. They run in circles working on some environmental horror of progress, e.g., a migraine, inability to breathe, trying to take everything in at once—"Cookie Monster Eyes" . . .*

LOVER: *(Sings)* This is the price we pay for progress in the world today.

RUNNER *runs to* LOVER, *rips off quilt and runs with it in front of her.*

RUNNER: *(On platform, very cocky to audience)* Don't, don't work, Don't, don't eat,
Don't breathe the air from the sky above.
(Crosses downstage to RUNNER)
The only thing still healthy to do—

(Lunges behind heart quilt with RUNNER*)*
Stay under the covers and make, make love.
And a make, make love! And a make, make love!

RUNNER *and* LOVER *begin a mouth-to-mouth breath jam as they run behind the heart quilt, only heads showing. In this mouth-to-mouth breath jam which occurs twice in the piece, the actors involved should work on her/his own lovemaking breath rhythm and breathe it down their partner's thorat.*

MOTHER *runs in appearing on up right of platform. She is nibbling/ sampling apple-sauce. As she runs, she calls out to* RUNNER.

MOTHER: Have some applesauce, I just made it.

RUNNER: Not now, *(Still in mouth-to-mouth breath jam with* LOVER*)* I'm busy.

HUSBAND *transforms into a dog who, with other dogs (played by other members of the ensemble) see* RUNNER *and* LOVER, *chase them and rip off the quilt. They are shocked and cover themselves.* LOVER *runs off.* RUNNER *runs to her* MOTHER.

MOTHER: *(Very involved in her own eating)* You have to eat sometime.

RUNNER: You put sugar in your applesauce.

MOTHER: Just a pinch.

RUNNER: *(Hanging arms and torso)* It'll weigh me down.

MOTHER: Applesauce!

RUNNER: The sugar.

MOTHER: *(The first time she really relates to her daughter)* You didn't expect me to use Saccharin!

RUNNER: I don't need any.

MOTHER: I don't see how you can expect to win on "Gator-Ade."

The other actors run in from left and right and perform images of runners crossing the finish line. The image is held momentarily as if it were a photo finish. These finishes may be triumphant, exhausted, exhilarated, etc. The image is held, then the actors move to another position in the performing area and strike another photo finish image. These continue.

RUNNER: I don't drink that, either.

MOTHER: *(As she digs in her real soft-sculpture or mimed ditty bag)* I'm not going to feed you raw meat.

RUNNER: You don't have to. I ate my quota this morning.

MOTHER: *(Still digging in bag)* The next thing you know, it'll be tapeworm.

RUNNER: *(Exasperated)* Mother!

MOTHER: *(She pulls out a soft-sculpture battery-operated shaver, holds it high and flips it on, making the sound of the shaver. She zeros in on RUNNER'S very unshaven legs.)* Bzzzzzzzzzzz!

RUNNER: *(Running away. She runs in place, but faster)* Stop it!

MOTHER: That's what I intend to do. *(Buzzing stops.)* These shorts are too short. I can see all the way to China.

RUNNER: Please just run with me a while. It'll help your diet.

MOTHER: *(Turning to side, sucking in cheeks)* I've decided to starve.

RUNNER: Running's easier.

MOTHER: Not for me.

RUNNER: *(Embracing her)* I love to have you with me. Will you run with me in the Spring Cross Country?

MOTHER: *(Gazing off into the distance)* I have to visit your sister, I won't have time to train. *(She follows her gaze and runs off to upper platform)*

The others break from photo finish images, using MOTHER running off as a catalyst. They all run to upper platform. Here, they become a row of "Cookie-Monster-Eyed" spectators. Their eyes move in circles and up and down, looking everywhere at once. Their feet move—toes together/heels out, heels together/toes out, propelling immobile bodies sideways across the platform. This device is used to create the illusion that RUNNER is running and the spectators are standing still.

RUNNER *upset and distracted by previous scene with her* MOTHER, *she runs in profile, looking after her* MOTHER *who exited left.*

FRIEND: *(Breaking out of photo finish, running toward* RUNNER *waving and full of love for her friend)* Hi.

RUNNER: *(Waving over her shoulder, she pulls herself together so she can relate to her friend)* Hi.

FRIEND: I've missed you.

RUNNER: Me, too.

FRIEND: I can't keep it up the way you can, but I do want to support you. *(Catching up to* RUNNER, FRIEND *uses her hand as a support under* RUNNER'*s bottom. They run like this in silence for a few beats.* FRIEND *falls slightly behind)* You're looking good. We drove up to the leading runners, and some are getting tired, and one fellow from Canada had a stitch in his side, and had to lie down on the River Road.

RUNNER: I'm not racing the men.

FRIEND: I just thought you'd like to know.

RUNNER: *(Changes direction, now runs front toward audience)* Thanks. *(A very awkward silence)*

FRIEND: *(Changes to small talk)* Are you tired of racquetball? *(She begins to run as if playing an easy game of racquetball which she continues through next lines)*

RUNNER: I just don't have as much time for it as I used to.

FRIEND: I admire your determination, but isn't racquetball more fun?

RUNNER: It's fun, but I don't think it's more fun.

FRIEND: *(Runs and swings at the racquet ball, becomes ferocious)* I can get rid of all my aggressions in racquetball.

RUNNER: *(Shocked at* FRIEND'*s aggressive behavior)* That's great. *(Runs right)*

FRIEND: *(Running behind* RUNNER*)* You know, not everyone can keep it up like you can.

RUNNER: *(Over her shoulder)* They don't have to.

FRIEND: A lot of our group is saying you're upping the peer pressure.

RUNNER: I don't know what you're talking about.

FRIEND: They're *not* going to run, just because you *are*.

RUNNER: I should hope not.

FRIEND: Well, they're not. They have their tennis clothes all bought for the season. *(Runs out, joins the other actors as a spectator on top platform)*

Spectators gesture wildly, while chanting urgently, breathless, "Run, run, run, run, run; run, run, run, run, run!" This chant continues throughout the dialogue and throughout the introduction to "Why Do You Run?" If one or more spectators stops chanting to speak, the others must continue the chant. RUNNER *runs in her second wind, profile toward stage left.* LOVER *enters behind a larger-than-life soft sculpture of a blond, tanned, female runner. The sculpture wears a beanie and bright running clothes and shoes that seem winged. It races with* RUNNER. *During the following lines, the spectators call out their lines, gesturing wildly, cheering the runners on.*

SPECTATOR 1: Lookin' good!

SPECTATOR 2: Get a horse!

SPECTATOR 3: Lookin' good!

SPECTATOR 4: You can run on my road any time!

SPECTATOR 1: Lookin' good!

SPECTATOR 4: Can I throw you one of my rocks?

SPECTATOR 2: Lookin' good!

SPECTATOR 1: Wouldn't you really rather ride the bus?

SPECTATOR 3: Lookin' good.

RUNNER *and soft sculpture female race nose to nose, vying for front position.*

BEANIED BLONDE: *(Soft sculpture, falsetto voice by* LOVER*)* Run here often?

RUNNER: Whenever I can.

BEANIED BLONDE: Your shoes are hot!

RUNNER: Your top is hot.

BEANIED BLONDE: Look at that hunky guy.

RUNNER: Where?

BEANIED BLONDE: *(In his own voice, peeking out from behind sculpture)* Here.

RUNNER: What?

BEANIED BLONDE: I'm going to catch up with him. *(In a burst of speed,* BEANIED BLONDE *runs off, leaving* RUNNER *in her dust)* Happy cruising!

RUNNER: *(Calling after her)* See you in L.A.—the 1984 *Women's* Marathon.

LOVER *puts down soft sculpture and rejoins the other spectators.* RUNNER *continues her steady pace in profile toward left.*

SPECTATOR 1: Hey, it's a UFO!

SPECTATOR 2: Unidentified Female Object?

SPECTATOR 4: No, Dork, it's a U *S* O!

SPECTATOR 5: Unidentified Sex Object!

MOTHER *runs down ramp from spectator image. Spectators continue* "Run, run, run, run, run!" RUNNER *runs toward audience.*

MOTHER: *(Overjoyed, bragging about her success)* The pins are working.

RUNNER: I don't want to hear about it.

MOTHER: *(Rejoicing)* Your father collapsed at work today.

RUNNER: I told you, I don't want to hear about it.

MOTHER: *(Cheering)* They have him up in intensive care.

RUNNER: *(Grabs* MOTHER, *confronts her)* Why aren't you there?

MOTHER: *(Her head on* RUNNER's *breast, fighting tears)* I was there, all night. *(She lifts her head and takes a big breath of air, beats her breast, fully recovered)* I just came out for a breath of air. *(Runs off to join spectators on upper platform)*

The spectators continue the "run, run" chant. Each transforms into character of HUSBAND LOVER, MOTHER, *and runs to* RUNNER *asking/demanding to know "Why do you run–" each returns to upper platform before hearing* RUNNER'S *response. On upper platform they become spectators, or* MOTHER, HUSBAND, LOVER, FRIEND, SPOKES-PERSON *as spectators.* RUNNER *continues running in place toward audience. The following lines are chanted in rhythm. (See musical score.)*

MOTHER: Why do you run?

RUNNER: I like to eat.

HUSBAND & LOVER: Why do you run?

RUNNER: To massage my feet.

FRIEND: Why do you run ?

RUNNER: To feel my heart beat.

SPECTATOR: Why do you run?

RUNNER: For fun!

ALL SPECTATORS: Run? *(Chant stops)* Why do you run?

RUNNER: For fun!

SPECTATOR-CHORUS: *(Singing, bearing down on* RUNNER, *running very low to ground)* Why do you run?

RUNNER: *(Sings)* I like to eat.

SPECTATOR/CHORUS: *(running with bulging belly, arms dangling behind)* Why do you run?

RUNNER: To massage my feet.

SPECTATOR-CHORUS: *(Mocking her, limp wrists high in air)* Why do you run?

RUNNER: To feel my heart beat.

SPECTATOR-CHORUS: *(Opening arms)* Why do you run?

RUNNER: For fun!

SPECTATOR-CHORUS: *(They stop running, puzzled, and sing)* Why do you run?

SPECTATORS *look at* RUNNER *and, as if by accident, bump bellies in pairs.*

SPECTATORS: Why do you run?

RUNNER: To heal my skin.

SPECTATOR-CHORUS: *(Still looking at* RUNNER. *Still in pairs, as if by accident, back into one another)* Why do you run?

RUNNER: To stay nice and thin.

SPECTATOR-CHORUS: *(Still in pairs, connect bodies, i.e., shoulder to belly, head to chest and run in a tight circle)* Why do you run?

RUNNER: I've just begun.

SPECTATOR-CHORUS: *(They stop, puzzled, and sing)* Why do you run? *(Dangling arms from the waist)* Why do you run?

RUNNER: Does there have to be an answer?

SPECTATOR-CHORUS: *(Boxing the air)* Why do you run?

RUNNER: To stay ahead of cancer.

SPECTATOR-CHORUS: *(Simple run)* Why do you run?

RUNNER: *(She begins to flap her arms)* 'Cause I can't fly.

The SPECTATORS *also begin to flap/fly, each in their own style.*

SPECTATOR-CHORUS: *(while running and flapping their arms)* Why do you run?

RUNNER: To get high!

SPECTATOR-CHORUS: *(Stop running and sing—)* Why?— Why?— Why?— Why, why? *(They demand, beginning the chant very loudly and gruffly, getting softer and more urgent as the "Why—High's" progress)* Why?— Why?— Why?— Why, why? Why?

RUNNER: High!

SPECTATOR-CHORUS: Why?

RUNNER: High!

SPECTATOR-CHORUS: Why?

RUNNER: High!

SPECTATOR-CHORUS: Why?

RUNNER: High!

SPECTATOR-CHORUS: *(Catching on)* Ohhhhhhhhh!!

RUNNER: *(Simultaneously with "Ohhhhhhhhh!!")* Hiiiiiiiiiigh!!
(Running and leaping) High!— High!— High!— High, *high!*

RUNNER & SPECTATORS: Run!— Run!— Run!— Run, *run!*
Run!— Run!— Run!

During the following the SPECTATORS *turn stage right and on each*
"get high," selects her/his own image of "getting high" and performs
each as a quick-change image isolation.

RUNNER & SPECTATORS: *(Sing)* Why do we run?
To get high,
Get high,
Get high,
To get high!
*(*SPECTATORS *jump off platform and shout with* RUNNER*)* Run!!!

Clicking noises on woodblock. The ensemble begins work on a noctur-
nal "paranoid run" back on the platform and ramp. On own, when
an actor hears a noise or feels someone or thing behind, stops, listens,
and looks. (The stops are not in unison.) What is seen, imagined or
real, affects the way the run is continued. Each stops, responds to
sound, and begins a new run.

RUNNER *runs in profile, through imagined dark alleys which trans-*
form into jungles with hanging vines which transform back into lonely
streets. LOVER *leaves the ensemble and runs down the ramp to*
RUNNER. *He follows some distance behind her, enjoying her derrière*
as she runs. Thinking lusty thoughts, he gets up his courage to
approach her.

LOVER *coming up quickly behind her, attempts an embrace.*

RUNNER *startled, changes her direction. She runs toward the audience.*

LOVER: How about a quickie under the bridge?

RUNNER: *(Freeing herself)* Not now.

LOVER: You used to like matinees.

RUNNER: I'm engaged.

LOVER: You're married.

RUNNER: So are you. *(The physical distance between* LOVER *and* RUNNER *grows.)*

LOVER: *(Runs toward audience, stage left;* RUNNER, *stage right)* Are you doing this to stay away from me?

RUNNER: Your self-indulgence is only surpassed by your sex appeal.

LOVER: *(Opens his arms toward her)* Ahhhh! Ahhhh! *(He lunges toward* RUNNER*)* Ahhhh! You still love me! (RUNNER *just barely escapes his arms by running stage left.* LOVER *regains his dignity and joins* RUNNER*)*

RUNNER: I've found it's necessary to look ahead.

LOVER: It's more fun in the moment.

RUNNER: It's more fun for you to talk.

LOVER: *(Over her shoulder)* What do you see ahead? *(He lifts* RUNNER *upward from behind. She wraps her legs around his waist, image of a ship's masthead or Moses on the mountain top)*

RUNNER: I see myself as—Moses!

LOVER: Then climb *my* mountain!

The other actors and LOVER *and* RUNNER *transform into "animal-self breathing" image.* LOVER *and* RUNNER *are the catalyst for this change. The animal breathing image is giving voice to the animal part of each actor.*

MOTHER: *(She breaks from the animal pack and runs downstage to* LOVER *and* RUNNER *who remain in "Moses" image)* I bought some "Nieman Marcus" stickpins.

All continue animal breathing.

RUNNER: Oh, for presents?

Animal breathing continues.

MOTHER: *(Crossing conspiratorially in front of* LOVER/RUNNER *to stage left)* No!—to stick in your father.

*All the actors as animals gasp, throw up their paws/wings in shock,
then run as their animal-selves around the playing area. As* LOVER
gasps, he drops RUNNER *and joins the animal run. After animal run
is established on both sides of* RUNNER—*who is running center stage
and transforming into her many animal-selves—the ensemble drops
to the ground on both sides of* RUNNER, *foreheads to the earth, they
massage their lower backs.*

RUNNER: Watch the feet—

*The actors, in unison, place hands on ground and look front—silence
as all watch the feet.*

RUNNER: Travel up front of the eye. No—!

Actors rise as SPECTATORS.

RUNNER: If think about feet, fall on nose—

Actors as SPECTATORS, *cheer on imagined numbers of runners,*
RUNNER *is amongst these. They wildly gesture with upstage arms,
opening and closing their jaws with their downstage hand. They breath
out audible sounds. The opening and closing jaw makes this sound
like excited crowd gibberish. The actors use* RUNNER'S *speech, and
the silence within it, to conduct the rises and falls in volume, pitch,
and dynamics of their gibberish.*

RUNNER: *(She continues with a very rhythmic run, chanting rhythmi-
cally)*
Don't think about the feet.
Head up, *(she throws her head up and tucks her chin)*
Elbows churnnnnnnnnnn!
The heart is a pump.
My heart. Sweet heart. Bleeding heart.
Hustle the muscle—
(Name calling) The legs are a pump for the heart chump.
(A warning, RUNNER *jumps, avoiding an obstacle or bump in the
road. She breaks her rhythm.)* Chump—
Watch out for the —B—
(reestablishing her rhythm) Back to the rhythm. Don't look at the
ground. I'll fall. Like my horse. Hooves over my nose, into a
mole hole. *(In silence, except for the maintained rhythm of her feet)*
It isn't ground,
It's cement.

Get back on the ground.
(Rubbing bone up lower leg) I'm gonna get shin splints.
There must be a way—to get in touch with the body—
Without thinking about the heart.
My heart.
But why do I have to run if my heart is good?
I don't
I can quit whenever I want to,—
　　But I don't want to quit. I love it!
If I'm lucky enough to have a small heart
I'm going to keep her drowning in blood;
　　She loves it! She loves it!
　　So much oxygen in the blood wash.
The more red corpuscles,
The more oxygen
can get to my heart
If I stay on the traaaaaaail!!

SPECTATORS, *in unison, cheer on a favorite runner.* RUNNER *runs down ramp to downstage center, she addresses the audience in confidence. She maintains her rhythmic run.*

RUNNER: Maybe I should have bought red tennis shoes.
I love red tennis shoes.
But 'fraid color too vivid—
will distract eye
　　during ruuuuuuuuuuuuuun!!

Actors, with great force, run at a partner; an image of the childhood competitive game of holding off your opponent by placing an extended arm on his forehead and urging him to hit/swing at you. This image is used to show competitive runners. Actor-partners run at one another while holding a partner at arm's length. Each pair decides when to switch leaders. The leader is the one doing the holding. To change, the other of the pair ducks away, extends her/his arm and the leader changes. If there is an uneven number of actors, the extra actor may continue the image of the gibberish spectator throughout this segment. RUNNER *changes direction to profile, continuing confidential tone with audience.*

RUNNER: Which bank of the Missouri
am I running on?

The east bank? Or the west bank?
(Gesturing ahead of her) Since I'm heading south—
Must be—
West bank.
(Leaping over obstacles, maintaining rhythm) Watch out for land mines! *(Ducking, holding ears, dodging grenades whizzing through the air)* Look out for hand grenades. *(Looking toward the sky)* There flies a crow carrying a plastic bomb? *(A crack on woodblock)*

Bluesy, boogie music begins, vibrational tremors shoot through RUN-NER *several times during next speech. The actors continue competitive run image, while leaping over cracks and crevices in the earth.*

RUNNER: This earthquake is seven point two on the Richter scale— But I can *(Jump, tremor)* jump, these cracks *(Jump)* in the earth—
As fast as I can heal
the ones
in my head. *(She begins a laid-back boogie run to the music)*

The paired actors back up to separate and join RUNNER *center stage in boogie run. The "pack run" image from the beginning of the play is repeated. There the actors vie with one another for a front position and show their responses as they find themselves at the back of the pack. Here their attitude is very playful/mischievous. They run and vie for position to the boogie beat like leprechauns.* RUNNER *and* HUSBAND *boogie-run backwards up ramp to upper platform.* HUS-BAND *is winded (a repeated emblem of his character) but gives* RUNNER *a hard time about falling behind the others. The actors divide into two groups, downstage right and left. In these smaller groups, they continue to boogie-run and vie.*

HUSBAND: *(Fighting for breath—an attempt to discourage her)* There's more than ten ahead of you.

RUNNER: *(Enjoying herself)* That's fine.

HUSBAND: *(Putting his arms over her shoulders like a coach)* I know you're just competing against yourself, but . . .

RUNNER: *(Running with him, disentangling herself, she runs down ramp)* Did you put the dinner in the microwave?

HUSBAND: Yes.

RUNNER: *(Playfully running ahead and calling over her shoulder)* Don't forget to eat it.

HUSBAND: *(Catching up to her)* I'm not like you. The kids and I won't forget to eat. *(Leaning on her/nudging her/applying physical-emotional pressure)* Listen— I don't want to pressure you, but . . .

RUNNER: *(Removing his hands, moving away from him)* Out with it.

HUSBAND: *(He pressures her)* Well, it wouldn't hurt . . .

RUNNER: *(Joking with him)* The pressure's building.

HUSBAND: *(Blurts)* It wouldn't hurt for you to win once in a while.

RUNNER: *(In all confidence, she sings)* If I win, I win. If I don't, I don't.

HUSBAND: *(Dangling a soft-sculpture carrot)* There's prizes.

RUNNER: I'm doing this for myself—I don't care about anything else.

Actors run off.

HUSBAND: *(Urging)* Since they're there anyway, you could just put on some speed at the end . . .

RUNNER *turns to* HUSBAND, *takes him firmly by the shoulder, turns him so they face one another.*

RUNNER: Just give me my vitamins and shut up.

They begin image of mouth-to-mouth breath jam. They continue this jam throughout the next dialogue. When RUNNER *responds to a line of dialogue, the mouth-to-mouth image continues and* HUSBAND *continues breath.*

FRIEND: *(Circles* RUNNER *and* HUSBAND *downstage and runs off)* Why do you run so much these days?

RUNNER: Playing drums isn't enough.

SPOKESPERSON: *(Circles* RUNNER *and* HUSBAND *downstage as a concerned, interested relative)* Why don't you get a nice job in a college somewhere, teaching? *(Runs up ramp to upper platform)*

RUNNER: For the same reason you don't join the Nazi party.

Musical introduction to "Blah to Running" begins. The ensemble runs in, each runs onto the playing area for a slow motion/determined run. Each runs in own style. All are very low to the floor to avoid the wind factor. The music for the first section of this song should be exaggerated, slow and monotonous.

SPOKESPERSON: *(Lounging on upper platform, she sings very laid back and pleased to be that way)*
I say blah to running,
Baaaaah to swimming,
Boo to bicycles,
And yuck to all this physical fitness,
It's giving me the pitsness.
(Slowly rises) Look at the time it takes.
I could bake a dozen devil's food cakes
In the time it takes.
I could drink fifty malted milk shakes
In the time it takes.

Tempo of music picks up. The actors form a line in profile toward stage right. They run forward waving gleefully.

SPOKESPERSON: I could write the great American novel

Actors remain in the same line, but back up in unison.

SPOKESPERSON: Or redecorate my hovel

Actors turn front and run in place, legs flying behind them.

SPOKESPERSON: In all the time it takes

Actors run in a circle, closely following each other.

SPOKESPERSON: To run around the track with all you flakes

The actor at the head of the line leads the others up ramp, they take places around SPOKESPERSON.

SPOKESPERSON: While you're out running in the snow
(Using the actors as covers) I'm snuggled down in my covers,
Rocking with the planet waves
And going with the flow.

Actors exercise on ramp and upper platform, each choosing the physical warmup that best shows off her/his skills.

SPOKESPERSON: I don't want to grow into Arnold Schwartzenegger
Or Diana Nyad.
I don't give a piffle to see my muscles ripple;
I'm a natural-born sedentary mole.
Longevity has never been my goal.

The lights dim. The actors transform into inhabitants of a sleazy, smoke-filled club. They regroup lounging over/around/about the SPOKESPERSON.

SPOKESPERSON: I want to live in the golden glow
Of cigarette smoke,
And turkey gravy—
With more, more, more full flavor.
What good is a perfect body
In an atomic war?

Blackout

In this blackout, the actors find images of Greek/Roman archetypal male and female athletes.

They are not frozen poses, they are living images momentarily stopped in the midst of physical activity, e.g., the moment of throwing a javelin.

Lights up.

SPOKESPERSON: You never know how long we'll be here,
So while you're out running,
I'll drink all the beer, all the beer that is here.
All I want is a life of good cheer.

Actors run down the ramp to playing area floor. They run like steam engines, puffing little explosions from their mouths. The image is of runners following too closely to the rear of a bus. They make these little cough explosions in order to breathe. They run very low to the ground in an attempt to escape the fumes.

SPOKESPERSON: I'm not afraid of the bell's toll,
Longevity has never been my goal.
Bartender, please bring me another schooner of beer,
    and fill my pipe,

There is too much fresh air in here!

Now everyone does a four-minute "transformational run," transforming, each in own time, to different people running in different situations and environments. This run is performed on four physical levels:
1. *Standing and running, feet leaving the floor.*
2. *Torso run, standing and running, feet never leave the floor.*
3. *A torso run on the knees.*
4. *A run on hands and knees.*
During (1) the actors may run to another position in the playing area. During (2), (3), (4), the only movement is up or down, actors remain in the same playing area position. The actors move through these levels and back through the duration of the run. As the character/place/situation-activity transformation occurs to each actor, an emotional response to each new situation affects a change in the breath rhythm. The audibleness of the breathing and the changes in breath rhythm are critical to this run and are present throughout the run—they create a breath jam, e.g., a soldier running on the combat field, Peter Rabbit running home after visiting Farmer McGregor's garden.

At the end of four minutes, MOTHER *breaks from the transformational run, runs to* RUNNER, *grabs her as if rescuing her from a fate worse than death. The others silently remain on the physical level and with character/situation image on which they were working when* MOTHER *speaks.*

MOTHER: *(Grabs* RUNNER *by the shoulders)* I want you to get a cancer policy. You might need intensive care.

RUNNER: *(Somewhat breathless and taken aback by* MOTHER's *suggestion—a pause)* I miss my dogs and cats. That's the only thing I don't like about running.

MOTHER: Your dogs could run with you.

RUNNER: *(A pause)* They'd bark and nip at the other runners.

MOTHER: All the better for you.

RUNNER: *(A pause)* But it isn't fair.

MOTHER: Is it fair to leave them in the house while you run? *(She runs off.* RUNNER, *deeply confused, runs to upper platform)*

Woodblock beats of 5/4 time begin. The actors rise, run to the sides of playing area and return with percussion instruments with which they beat 5/4 time. They form a group downstage right and begin a unison "paranoid run." One of the actors is the leader, (s)he reacts to a shadowy sound or vision and stops, all actors stopping in unison with her/him. Each listens, and (in own time) run-turns (each in own rhythm) around to see what the sound or shadow was and continues. Each continues with an individual run created as a result of what each runner saw or didn't see and their emotional response to it. During the "paranoid run" a soft-sculpture bear joins RUNNER. *They run together on the lower platform. After several stops,* LOVER *leaves the group and runs to the upper platform where he discovers* RUNNER *with the bear. He frightens the bear away.* LOVER *and* RUNNER *run side by side on upper platform. The "paranoid run" and 5/4 percussion beats continue throughout the following dialogue.*

LOVER: I've been evicted.

RUNNER: Again?

LOVER: I don't know how she found out.

RUNNER: What did she find?

LOVER: Shit in the kitchen.

RUNNER: Yours?

LOVER: Hers.

RUNNER: She shat in your kitchen?

LOVER: My girlfriend's dog shat in *her* kitchen.

RUNNER: You can't blame the dog.

LOVER: It wasn't my dog.

RUNNER: That's just my point.

LOVER: I don't get it.

RUNNER: *(They separate, facing each other and take long walk/run strides backwards to extreme sides of upper platform)* Why didn't you walk the dog?

LOVER: The dog walked itself.

RUNNER: I want romance, and you bring me dog doo-doo.

LOVER: It's not my dog.

RUNNER: It is your girlfriend.

LOVER: *(Opening arms to her—running close to her and away from her with arms open—it is as if she is in his arms one moment, and an independent spirit the next)* I'm in love with *you*.

"Paranoid" runners break to sidelines to put down instruments.

RUNNER: That's dangerous.

LOVER: Why?

RUNNER: I have *two* dogs.

All, including RUNNER *and* LOVER, *run onto downstage playing area forming a semicircle center stage. They are runner/jocks who hurt, are competitive, and are envious of each other. They cynically chant and run.*

CHORUS OF RUNNERS: *(Chant)* What do you *do*,
(A quick, competitive look over right shoulder)
Who do *you*
(Another look) do,
(Another look) What
(A shrug) do you do
(Torso and arms hang, gesture toward feet)
When your feet's so beat
(Reach toward audience) You can't
(An isolation pull back) make your ends meet?
(Arms wildly moving like doing a swimming stroke)
You fly through your drool.
(A very determined run, arms pumping)
You keep right on running
(Hits self in jaw with fists)
Like a running fool,
(Arms above head, wrists limp. Image of "Running Is for Sissies")
Like a running fool.
(Actors run, arms above heads, wrists limp, they chant "running fool," then move their heads—chant and mockingly move foolishly)
Running fool,

Running fool,
Running fool,
Running fool . . .

FRIEND *breaks from the semicircle. Others continue chanting "running fool" under first four lines of her solo.*

FRIEND: *(Sings)* Oh, I knew a lady so pink and fine,
She had translucent skin.
Lived on oysters and white wine,
Lived on oysters and white wine.

Actors hiss, boo, make obscene gestures at other runners ahead of them—they are very poor sports. Through the following, RUNNER *moves from semicircle to* FRIEND.

FRIEND: But when I came by
She leapt up with a sigh
and—
(FRIEND surprises RUNNER, who squeals) Yelled!!!

FRIEND *and* RUNNER *hug, cheer and congratulate each other. Other actors show their jealousy of* FRIEND, RUNNER, *and everyone else in the race. The actors chant cynically.*

FRIEND *and* RUNNER *chant supportively. Throughout the following they run and hug one another. They run, literally, nose to nose—rubbing noses, they hold hands and run, they dance and run. the following actions are performed by the others, through gritted teeth.*

CHORUS OF RUNNERS: *(Snob, looking down noses)*
You're looking good.
(Close to ground, speed race) You're looking good,
(Sticking in knife) You're looking good,
(Holding their heads) You stubborn mule.
(Beating breasts—"Mea Culpa") You're looking good.
(Regular run, arms pumping, limp wrists) You're a running fool.
(Tempo picks up, actors run faster) You're looking good,
You're looking good,
You're looking good
Like you know you should.
You're looking *good,*
(A paranoid look over shoulder) You're looking *good,*
(A paranoid look over shoulder)

(Name call) You Omaha mule!
(Turn backs on them, run in profile toward right)
You're a running fool!
(Turn heads front, torso run, feet do not leave the floor, longingly sung) You're looking good,
You're looking good,
(Stop running, sung with hate) You running
(Jump front and shout) Fool!!

All except RUNNER *break to stage left, making wind-in-trees whistling sounds. Lights dim.* RUNNER *runs in profile. All alone she recalls, lovingly, from her past. The actors put on soft-sculpture trees on the sidelines, with their backs to the audience.*

RUNNER: I miss my twin
     but I feel certain she's running with me.
She's my guardian angel
        flying over me
        at all times.
This is a good place
        to get close to her;
When I run
        it's like we're having fun
                    again,
Like we did
        in Mother's ocean,
        or we could have
            if she had lived.

Actors turn and enter as soft-sculpture trees. They find the particular rhythm true to each tree, i.e., a willow moves much differently than a thick, sturdy oak. RUNNER *runs in place. The trees rush by behind her to give the illusion that she is moving. Each cross they make from left to right is in a definite pattern, e.g., one tree, then another, several feet behind; then another, several feet behind that one . . . Or: A clump of trees in a grove; or two trees, side by side, then a single willow . . . The possibilities are infinite. On their return to stage left, the trees sneak, in profile, on tip toe, behind* RUNNER, *as if they are invisible.*

RUNNER: She would have been my older sister,
Born dead.

Mother was so sad
But Grandma said,
   "I know you're not finished,
   Stand on your head,
I know you're not finished,
Listen to your mother,
Don't lift your head
   from that bed.
I know you're not finished,
   the doctor's Mashuganah,
   God sent you a living baby,
     have patience
     don't move
       let the blood flow up,
       run past the pain,
Stand on your head
   for just six more months.
Lay there
   and pray
     for your child."

Weeping willow tree moves to RUNNER, *surrounds her with its branches. The other trees move to positions in the playing area.* RUNNER *turns front and shares the following confidence with the audience.*

RUNNER: And sure enough,—
I popped out running!
And Mother rolled me
   in the new grass;
   "A Spring child is the best child to have
   and I took you outside
   and I showed you how
    the grass grew,
   and the first
      little green sprouts
      came up with you,
   and the first April showers
     fell
     on your tongue,
   and we went into the fields

         to drink milk
         from the moo cows *(Trees slowly begin to exit)*
            with their calves,
      and we chased
         the woolly lambs."
And Mother roared like a little dog
         while the moon
                  jumped over
                     Omaha.

The trees/wind/whistling has ended. There is silence. RUNNER *runs toward audience alone with her memories.*

We've got the biggest moon
      in the world
      in Nebraska,
         it's gotta be—
to go with our sky.

That's why
      I run now,
I've spent so much time
      on my back
            looking at the sky—

Bizarre, unidentifiable animal noises are created by the actors from the sidelines. They should not be recognizable animal sounds, i.e., no dog, cow or bird sounds.

RUNNER: I've turned into a prairie porpoise;
And I sing with the prairie grasses,
And sling spit shots into
      spiders' webs, *(She runs with great difficulty, dangling arms hanging from the torso)*
And I must grow my arms and legs
      again—

The actors continue animal sounds. Two actors, as they continue animal sounds, run to RUNNER, *sink to the ground, and place great weight on* RUNNER's *feet—each holds an ankle.* RUNNER, *exhausted, continues to push herself and run.*

Pump
Pump

Pump
Pump—
   these legs
     my legs
I wonder
if I could
   run faster
If I'd stayed down
   on all fours
     from childhood?
These hands
That used to swing from trees
   are no good
    for anything
     now
But pouring tea.

The two ankle-holders exit.

LOVER: *(Runs in, leaps on her back, covers her eyes, and disguises his voice)* How do you know I'm not a rapist?

RUNNER: *(Feels his feet)* You're wearing Adidas.

LOVER: May I call on you?

RUNNER: Don't soft-soap me. I'm running hard.

LOVER: I'd like to take you out for a great gourmet feast.

RUNNER: I only eat raw meat.

LOVER: I'll take you to the zoo. *(Jumps off her back and exits)*

Animal noises stop.

RUNNER: Sort of cute—shall I race him? No—I'm only racing myself.

Primitive drum beat begins. The actors run front always toward the audience, up and down the ramp and downstage area. They work on survival images of primitive runners. These may be one-person images or may involve two or more actors. RUNNER *runs down center.*

RUNNER: *(Startled at the vision)* There are the tracks of the ten-million-year-old hippopotamus. *(Her attention is pulled to another sight. She's surprised.)* There are the tracks of the fifteen-million-fifteen-year-olds.

The actors begin to feel pain, a cramp, in different parts of their bodies. They run through the pain until it dissolves or it gets the better of them and drags them down. During this section they run for survival.

RUNNER: *(A lament)* Oh, the cigarette butts. Oh, the filter tips.
    The wicked witch will find all of you—
  She has only to follow the trail of your filter tips.
(Another vision pulls her attention) There's the petrified feather of the pterodactyl. *(Looking up)*
    The hawk is hanging in the updraft *(One by one, each in his own time and way, the actors fall dead in a pile "Homage to Guyana" image)*
    Waiting for my carcass to quit . . .
It seems
    It seems
If I could just give myself the gun—
I could get up there
    Up there with the hawk.
This run's just a run—
A run on the ground;
    That hawk looks so omnipotent—

RUNNER *runs in silence. She has no more energy, it is as if she cannot go on, her arms hang, she has a stitch, she is winded, she can hardly speak.*

RUNNER: *(A fresh burst of energy)* A second wind
and this is what I like about keeping on.
Keep on   Keeping on
          and you get windborn again!

Silence, RUNNER *looks around.*

RUNNER: *(In confidence)* I have the foot path
         to myself.

Dirt,
I love running
      on dirt.
My gramma said

    "A little dirt
never hurt anybody."
When I was four
I ate a spoonful   of dirt
        a day

RUNNER *runs stage right and chants.*

RUNNER: I'm running to tell the Queen
I'm running to tell the Queen
I'm running to tell the Queen
The sky is bluer
    than it's ever been
(Runs stage left and chants)
I'm running to tell the King
I'm running to tell the King
I'm running to tell the King
The moon rides high
    inside a white ring.
(In confidence) My mother says the moon is closer to my
    heart in Omaha,
It's closer
Than at the equator,
It's closer
Than at the top of Mt. Rainier,
It's closer
    than in the Himalyayas;
(A cheer) we can be moon ruled
Here in Omaha!
She drooled
    and fled down the path—
(Eggs them on) Yes, yes, yes,
Hit me with a pail of
alligator pop,
(Ducking and running)
Bop
  Bop
    Bop
      Bop
(Open arms) Pour more *(Substitute local bottled water company)*
Fontenelle Forest spring water for me,

No Gator-Ade,
Give it to the jocks;
I'm a fake
I just love to run.
I'm trying hard
      to find the right shoes
      and shorts
      to wear,
But what I love best
Is to run   on dirt
         or in the mud.

Silence. RUNNER *switches to very slow motion "Tai Chi run," feeling the support of the earth, vibration from the earth and the air. She works with the image of finding the source of the run within her body. The following is recited as a meditative closing prayer.*

RUNNER: Where is this body—
Floating free 'round my bones.
Do the hurdy gurdy
or shimmy
at my sister Kate's
      rate.
I got a date
      with the trees,—
I'm gonna be
      the tree's breeze.

RUNNER *breaks the silence with the rhythm of her run. She rejoices in celebration.*

RUNNER: One day
if I run long enough
I will celebrate the marriage
      of my head
      and my body.
This seems to be
one of the major splits
of the twentieth century.
One can spend
      a lifetime
Trying

to get the head
        and body
to blend as one.
up 'til now
It's been
Bicker
    Bicker
        Bicker.

MOTHER *disengages herself from the other bodies. She runs to* RUN-
NER. *The pile of bodies separates, one by one as if reborn. Each actor,
stiff-legged, looks for his run. This image should examine the effort
of young children learning how to walk. "A walk is just like a run,
only slower." The actors continue in this "world of the last run"
through the next scene.*

MOTHER: *(Gleefully)* Your father's lost his voice.

RUNNER: Is he still in the hospital?

MOTHER: No, he went to the Islands.

RUNNER: Did he call you?

MOTHER: Not me—I told you he lost his voice. *(Giggling madly)*
Isn't it wonderful? *(Exaggerated horror)* He got a bug down his
throat in the Islands.

RUNNER: *(Embracing her)* Mother—stay with me. Run with me.
Let's be Ma Bell's ad on TV—two generations running together.

MOTHER: *(In her own world, she ignores* RUNNER, *moves away from
her and to the upper platform)* I have to work. The dollar is
having the dipsie-doodle knocked out of it. You're just like
your father—you pay yourself for playing. America is going
down the drain. The Japs and Germans are dumping Drano
by the tons on our heads. Do you think we can swim back out
if everyone's running to the woods and running to the Islands?
(In absolute confidence with the audience) The locusts are coming
again—*soon! (She exits)*

RUNNER: *(To the audience, reassuring)* Locusts are sixty-eight
percent protein.

All (entire company) do slow motion "cosmic runs" on floor area of performing space. The actors explore moon walk/weightless runs, explore off-balance runs, and basically have a good time, cosmically moving to the music. RUNNER, FRIEND, *and* SPOKESPERSON *are on upper platform.*

RUNNER: *(Sings)* I know I'm goin' when I'm goin'.

FRIEND: *(Sings)* I know I'm goin' when I'm goin'.

SPOKESPERSON: *(Sings)* I know I'm goin' when I'm goin'.

RUNNER, FRIEND & SPOKESPERSON: *(Sing)*
Gonna be the wind, gonna be the rain,
Gonna be the wind, gonna be the rain,
Gonna be the wind and the rain.

I know I'm goin' when I'm goin'.
I know I'm goin' when I'm goin'.

RUNNER: Gonna be the wind.

FRIEND: Gonna be the rain.

SPOKESPERSON: Gonna be the winning one in this race for one.

ALL THREE: I know I'm goin' when I'm goin'—
Shoobie doobie doobie doo!
I know I'm goin' when I'm goin'.
Goin' closer to the sun, closer to the sun,
    closer to the sun.
Gonna be the winner in this race for one.

And I won't be back
'Till I've run the cosmic track,
The cosmic track,
The cosmic track.

RUNNER & FRIEND: Cosmic, cosmic, cosmic, cosmic,
Cosmic, cosmic, cosmic, cosmic . . .
(Continue under SPOKESPERSON*)*

SPOKESPERSON: I know I'm goin' when I'm goin'.
I know I'm goin' when I'm goin'.

RUNNER: Gonna be the wind.

FRIEND: Gonna be the rain.

ALL THREE: Gonna be the winning one in this race for one.
I know I'm goin' when I'm goin'.

RUNNER & FRIEND: I know I'm goin' when I'm goin'.

FRIEND: I know I'm goin' when I'm goin'.

ALL THREE: I'm goin',
I'm goin', I'm goin', I'm goin', I'm goin',
    I'm goin', I'm goin', I'm goin', I'm goin',
    I'm goin'—
I'm go—in'!

END OF PLAY

APPENDIX: ORDER

This order may be posted on both sides of the performing area as a guide for new runners who may wish to perform in the piece. The list serves as a commedia dell'arte *structure outline so actors can attend to the business of performing without worry about "what comes next."*

Horn
Push run—to upper platform right
Conductor drop—animal run
Animal breathing
Second hold (alert) Howl
3 runs (chasing dinner—being chased)
3rd run in place
Torso run
Frightened breath
Look right, look left
2 actors leapfrog
Falcon scream
Line-up for spring 2 times
Dearest God—back massage
Run on knees (count 5)
Torso run (10)
Run
City Noise
Actors right left right
Pivot right to salesman scene—running in pairs
Breathing in and out—demonstration
I want you know the natural order—THE WILLS
Intensity song
I wish I wish
2 actors—showing bodies after duck's disease—actors exit
Hi, how you doin' *until* Eat, drink, and be merry, dance
Turn front—Sisyphus run
Drink this
Da da da—the groaners
Maybe I should have stuck with swimming—slow motion
It goes away when I dream—slowly toward PUDDLES
Why are you crying . . . to science
Pick Friend up, run, take pulse
Coal miner

Bears dance
Run down and get heart
I have the answer
Applesauce
Friend "Hi"—spectators
Run run run—spectator lines
Lover and Beanied Blonde soft-sculpture
More spectator lines
The pins are working
Run run run song
Paranoids on platform
How about a quickie
I adore arrogance—animal breaths
I bought some Nieman Marcus stickpins—father—GASP
Animal runs
Rub backs
Watch the feet travel up front—giggling chins—spectators
    gibberish
Pushruns holding head of person (color too vivid)
Animal run
Ten more ahead of you
Husband and Runner breathing mouth to mouth
Friend and Spokesperson run by with lines
Blah song
Breath runs (4 minutes) 8 bings and 1 bang
Cancer policy
Paranoids with instruments
I've been evicted
Why do you run
I miss my twin trees (SILENCE over Moon over Omaha)
Animal sounds That's why I run
2 actors as weights hold Runner's legs (Pump pump)
RAPIST
Tracks of 15 million 15-year-olds
Running back and forth on platform
Wicked witch—begin with pain and dropping to pile up
Footpath to myself—bicker bicker bicker
Father lost his voice—SEARCHING
I know I'm going

BABES IN THE BIGHOUSE

Book and Lyrics by Megan Terry
Structure by Jo Ann Schmidman
Music by John J. Sheehan

ENVIRONMENT

For the Omaha Magic Theatre production the playing area was a rectangular shape 10'x40'. This was dictated by the shape of our building. There were 2-3 rows of raised seating for the audience along the 40' sides. Double-decker cells for the inmates were constructed of metal scaffolding (which we painted bright yellows, reds, blues and greens) at one end of the playing area. At the O.M.T. the cells were at the entrance to the theater. The audience, upon entering and buying tickets, were immediately confronted with the cells, each individually outlined with 7½-watt Christmas tree lights. The small corridor leading to the seating area was roped off so that the audience was confined in the lobby.

While the audience waits, an audio tape plays. We made our tape by going door-to-door and asking people on the street questions about what they think goes on inside a women's prison. We found that the majority of responses were influenced by the gross amount of cheap sex novels, "grade C" drive-in movies and personal fantasies, all having to do with women locked up, as punishment, together. Therefore, the actors at O.M.T. were dressed in various combinations of corsets, long gloves, feathers and furs, garters, fish-net hose, spike heels and too much makeup.

Opposite the cells at the other end of the playing area is a six-inch-high platform (5'x 6'). A net hangs from the ceiling grazing the length of the platform. The net at O.M.T. was made from an old volleyball net. Affixed to the net were crocheted aprons, doilies and other articles which the prisoners made in crafts class. There is a 3' opening slit in the center of the net.

At various times in the play, the platform is used as the warden's office, the doctor's office and solitary confinement ("The Hole").

The area between the platform and the cells represents at various times—hallways, the shower room, the yard and the sewing room. The dominant dramatic image in the play is "how the women walk." They walk the halls from cells to laundry to cafeteria, etc.

As the actors/inmates walk through the hall, they focus their attention on the rhythms inside their heads.

The interior rhythms should be projected outward in the way each

individual walks. Each actor selects many characters to play through-
out the evening and this will be evident in the transformation of the
walks.

NOTE: Reasons for the interior are to maintain sanity, to withdraw
from others, to space out, to state who they are, etc., or to show
dominance or confusion as a guard.

When actors aren't involved in a scene with dialogue, at the director's
discretion they may continue the "walks."

The other dominant dramatic image in the play is the "imposing of
wills." Inmates impose wills on one another and on the guards. Several
weeks of workshop were spent working on "the wills." We discovered
when one imposed her will on another, the object of the will imposition
resisted. This created tension—a push/pull situation—and the image
was momentarily frozen until a guard came upon them, an inmate
approached or a prison noise would startle them. (These may be actual
or imagined.) This caused those involved in the imposing of wills to
pull away, change their focus, break the tension and thus change the
image, returning to "the walks."

O.M.T. never performs BABES *in proscenium. When we tour to a*
proscenium theater, we have all the audience seated on stage, in rows
of seats facing each other along the longest side of the stage (on a
deep, narrow stage, along the left and right of the playing area on
a wide, shallow stage, along the front and back). No one sits in the
"house." This does limit seating, but maintains the feeling of the
audience's being observers inside a prison.

COSTUMES

For Opening Section: The actors are dressed in the most extreme of the audiences' fantasies of how "bad girls" look. At the O.M.T. we used cheap prison novels, the covers of True Detective magazines and grade C women's prison movies as prime resources.

For the Body of the Play: The women prisoners were dressed in the simplest cotton housedresses and tennis shoes. When they transform into guards they slip on colorful band uniform jackets. When they transform into the visiting evangelists, they don old fashions and "proper" ladies' hats.

HOW WE DIVIDED THE PLAYING AREA
FOR STAGING AND LIGHTING AT THE O.M.T.

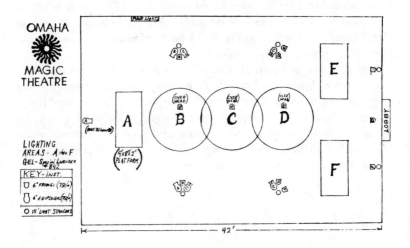

ACT ONE

The play begins. All twinkle lights twinkle up, as do playing area lights. The audio tape is turned off. The actors enter in extreme slow motion. They flirt with, seduce and try every available means to con the spectators. Gradually the audience members become aware of the actors who move toward them. They can only view the actors through the jail cells. Because of the physical setup, the audience has to work to see what is going on. As the actors enter their cells, the slow motion ends and each begins her opening monologue to con. Each actor speaks directly to various audience members trying to convince each one of her innocence.

When JOCKEY *begins to speak to the audience, twinkle lights on all cells remain on. Those lights on* JOCKEY'*s cell flash in rhythm to her speech. When* JOCKEY *takes focus, general light comes up on all cells.*

JOCKEY: Listen! You aren't gonna see what really goes on here. They'll have the whole place—and us—sanitized, de-loused, sterile, perfect and old-time Christian clean. They'll make you very happy with the way your tax dollars are being spent. Their lives depend on that, you bet! But make them show you the hole. They got a hole in here—they call it "The Adjustment Center." They want everything here to sound like a hospital or a school so you'll think that with a new name somethin's changed around here. No matter how many times they call it a "campus," this place is still a joint. You know what happens here? Nothing. Nothing. And then lots more of the same. They taught me how to fill a bucket with water and soap. Where to put my hands on the handle of a mop and how to tell the floor from the walls. When I get out of here, I get to be the best hotel maid in the world—but I'm allergic to detergent. Look at my hands—all the skin is peeling off.

*The lights continue to twinkle—*RONNIE *and* JOCKEY *are cellmates.*

RONNIE: Hi. How're you tonight? Welcome to our "campus."
It's such a nice drive on a clear day. I get into town often
lately. Some groups who're interested in us ask for me to come
and speak to them about how we're doing here. And believe
me, I'm glad to talk abut it. I've come a long way since I got
convinced I was my own worst enemy. I was doing hard time.
I was so mean I spent 49 days in the "Adjustment Center." I
wasn't about to change for nobody. But then it dawned on
me that the more I stayed in a negative vibration state, the
longer it would be till I could get back out into the free world.
I just had to turn myself around and become the other side
of the coin. For the first six months I had nothing but all the
shit jobs—scrubbing and scrubbing and then rubbing. When
it got dry they let me paint it—you know what I mean? But
now I've worked my way up to be head clerk of records here.
I'm saving my money. I got a bank account. I'm getting skills
I could use in an insurance company or any nice, clean business
like that. Now I'm doing easy time and looking forward to
joining you all one day soon. Loan me a cigarette?

Twinkle lights come up on CHAMP'S *cell. They remain on around*
RONNIE *and* JOCKEY'SS *cell.* RONNIE *exits to change to* MISS
SCHNAUZER.

CHAMP: Hello? You come with a tour group? Wanna play ball?
Got a good team here. El Toro bats 350, and that's on her
bad days. Listen, would you ask the Warden if she'll let you
take us swimming? I want to see something else. We get sick
of looking at each other. You roller skate? I was All State
Junior Champ in high school. They gave me up to two years
for possession. You believe it? Don't you think it's pretty silly
to spend all your money keeping me here for two jays? My
problem is I didn't think big enough . . . They pardon the big
guys, the really *big* guys. They got respect for the big guys.
Us little women, they bust us and throw away the key. I was
out riding in the first car I could ever afford to buy for
myself—had only two jays in my pocket. It was on the way to
get my inspection sticker. Lucky it was my first offense or I'd
have up to six. Cute, eh? Write your Congressman. I write
every day. If you don't have a record, they might even take

you seriously. Try it. Costs a hell of a lot of dough to keep
me here. I'd rather be surf fishing in San Clemente!

Lights twinkle around EL TORO'S *cell—stay on, on* CHAMP'S.

EL TORO: Nobody gonna rehabilitate *you!* You rehabilitate
yourself, y'understand? Like, if I'm sitting here and you tell
me to sit a certain way and look prim and proper like a
lady . . . I'm not gonna feel like doing that. That ain't me. I
like to sit and think, and I don't smile when I'm looking inside,
y'understand? Sometimes I get up in the morning, I want to
take a walk. I might want to talk to someone. But they don't
let you talk to anyone until after one p.m. on Saturday. They
got me trained to wake up at 6:30 a.m. *(Laughs, sputters)* I used
to go to *bed* at 6:30 a.m.! They got me working in the sewing
shop now, and I like it O.K. But when I first came here they
couldn't understand me. They don't realize that some of us
out there, *we don't work.* Not everybody has to do a nine-to-fiver
for chump change, y'understand. They write me up all the
time about my attitude. The matron always is looking at me
(demonstrates) when I'm like this, see—sitting and tripping on
myself—and she says, "What's wrong wit chew? You're not
happy!" *I'm* perfectly happy, *sitting here.* But around here they
want you always to be sitting like this *(she demonstrates a super-
perfect, little girl pose)* and grinning like an ape. Otherwise they
think you've gone mental! Like this babe we had in here. She
set fire to her mattress because they wouldn't let her hold
hands with the person she was sweet on. They sent her to
California. Told her she'd be happier there. Told her there
were no girls here like the "way" she was, y'understand? But
there were five hundred of them in the prison in California
and she wouldn't have to set fire to her mattress there.

Lights twinkle around KATHLEEN'S *cell—remain on* EL TORO'S.

KATHLEEN: I wouldn't work in a job where they can keep track
of you. You got to be out of your mind, honey. I know what
I'm talking about. My poor old mama, she worked in a square
job all her life. She worked as a waitress, she worked as a
florist. She had a trade, honey. You know what I mean—she
was an artist with flowers! When her arthritis got so bad she
couldn't make corsages and funeral sprays no more, she went

back into waitressing at Dunkin' Donuts. She worked all her
life—like since they invented Social Security—you dig? She
kept *all* her forms and she wrote down *all* her numbers, you
dig? She was always up front with her numbers. So she retires
two years ago. You know what the government gives her for
working from the time she was ten years old—you know what
they give her? Seventy-eight dollars a month. Count 'em.
Thanks a lot. Working fifty-five years, you dig? Fifty-five
years. How's she supposed to live on seventy-eight dollars a
month?? You figure it out. She'd be better off in here with us.

The sound rises fully as all prisoners now join with KATHLEEN
speaking key phrases from their speeches. All lights twinkle until MISS
SCHNAUZER, *a prison official, appears at opposite end of the playing
area. When the women see her, they fall silent and withdraw into
their darkened cells. During* MISS SCHNAUZER'S *speech they change
to prison dresses and tennis shoes. Over their dresses they wear identical
green or blue hospital or prison gowns.* MISS SCHNAUZER *wears a
gray and red guard coat. (In the Omaha Magic Theatre production,
when prisoners transformed to guards they slipped into bright marching band uniform jackets.)* MISS SCHNAUZER *unties the rope which
has kept the audience confined to the lobby. She shakes some hands,
welcoming them into the prison and directs them to seats. She smiles
to both sides of the audience, makes a gesture of welcome, stops, looks
down at the floor. She's not used to addressing so many people from
the free world at one time. She straightens up, works to relax her
body, her eyes showing inner disturbance. As she speaks she scans each
audience member very closely. She is checking to see that no contraband
(matches, cigarettes, a sharp object, a belt) is brought into the prison.
Years of watching for the passing of contraband and/or the tapping
of love messages on toes, keep her from letting go of the "guard" mind
set. She may be any age, but seems youthful and "with it."*

MISS SCHNAUZER: Hello there—I'm Miss Schnauzer, Assistant
to our Warden, in charge of working with the Parole Board,
the Legislature, and you—the community—and I want to
welcome you to our campus. I think some of you may have
noticed the new sign just to the right of the front gate:
"WOMEN'S STATE CORRECTIONAL FACILITY." The
legislature was kind enough to vote us a new name *this* year
and we were able to paint a new sign with materials left over

from repairing our "Adjustment Center." In the dark ages of penology, there *was* a place where inmates were confined for punishment, which our charges referred to as "solitary confinement," or euphemistically, as "the hole." But since the sociological-anthropo-sensitivity-psychiatric revolution has brought us into this new age of enlightenment—and thus more humane treatment geared toward rehabilitation—what *used* to be called "the hole" is now a gaily painted place where inmates who may be feeling upset may go to meditate— alone—away from the *hubbub* of correctional life.

She crosses to area in front of cells as she speaks. By this time most of the changing activity has been completed—at least all uncovering that the audience shouldn't see. As she crosses, lights follow her. They go out as she passes out of the area.

As East has met West, we in the West have been wise enough at times, I hope, to gear up and make use of some of the applicable Far Eastern personal development techniques which can be utilized in bringing sanity and calmness to some of our angrier ladies.

Distant growls and bar rattling noise from the cell areas. MISS SCHNAUZER *waits for it to end. She does not look at inmates but holds a smile on the audience.*

A few days of meditation and scientifically controlled fasting in "The Adjustment Center" helps a disturbed individual realize she'd rather have the company of her new friends here as well as three square meals a day. Further, I'd like to call your attention to the up-to-date plumbing. No woman has to flush a toilet herself. The flushing is controlled at the central guard station. This way one matron can supervise an entire cottage of girls, where it might have taken up to five before. This saves you, our employers and taxpayers, money in eliminated salaries. I'm really happy you were able to come today, as tensions sometimes run high here and seeing faces from the free world, faces of those who know how to live on the streets—I mean in ordinary society—can act as an inspiration to our girls.

As I'm sure you realize, by the time a girl is placed in here she's reached rock bottom. We work hard with the girls to help build up their self images, to teach them a trade so they may one day take their places as useful members of society. You'll hear various stories today. Please take most of them with the grain of salt. A lot of our girls have lived quite unreal lives and they do exaggerate their cases, and the reasons why they are here. But please understand me, we do show compassion for our girls, but *not* sympathy. You may feel at times that you want to show sympathy toward some of them, but let me caution you in advance: "sympathy is weakness." They won't respect you for it. They'll respect *you* if you respect *them*, but "sympathy is weakness," and they'll use every con game in the book to get you to fall for their stories. Thank you again for coming and showing an interest in what we're trying to do. We do need more money for staff and better facilities and you can help us toward these with your vote. And now we'll show you a composite picture of a day in the life of our facility. Please don't feed the inmates or ask to eat with us. Our budget doesn't cover you.

MISS SCHNAUZER *breaks into an enormous, toothy smile which freezes on her face. She rotates so that all the audience partakes of her good will. One prisoner comes out of her cell transformed to a GUARD wearing a blue and red jacket. She marches toward SCHNAUZER, who stands smiling and rotating. They perform a military "changing of the guard." The new GUARD lifts a violin to her shoulder and plays a dissonant chord to signify the prison bell. At sound of the chord, twinkle lights come up on cells and prisoners press noses to cell bars for count. Each prisoner, in an order established by the director, calls out a number from one to forty. These numbers vary from count to count.*

JOCKEY: Two

OX TAIL: Seven.

CHAMP: Sixteen.

EL TORO: Twenty-eight.

RONNIE: Thirty-six.

KATHLEEN: Forty.

GUARD *marches to cells and unlocks doors. (In Omaha Magic Theatre's production this was signified by hitting cell bars with a chain.) The prisoners (except* KATHLEEN, *who has been restricted) come out of their cells, stretching and yawning.* GUARD *moves to center playing area and mimes turning on showers. (In Omaha Magic Theatre's production the prisoners wore green surgical gowns as robes over their other costumes.) As they wait for their showers, the* GUARD *drags* KATHLEEN *from her cell and takes her to a shower way from the other women. During the following scene this* GUARD *takes a great deal of interest in* KATHLEEN'S *shower. Periodically,* KATH- LEEN *will catch the* GUARD *in the act of looking her up and down. The* GUARD *looks away just before their eyes meet. The other prisoners mime taking their showers (they do not remove their clothes).* RONNIE *showers with the rest, but listens and does not speak.*

Under the showers:

EL TORO: Got any kids?

CHAMP: Four. You?

EL TORO: Had two, but only know where one is.

JOCKEY: I got two. What happened to the other?

EL TORO: I don't know.

CHAMP: When'd you have it?

EL TORO: Reform school. I know it was alive. Right after birth I held her just for a minute. But then they knocked me out with something, and when I came to, they told me the baby died. I still don't believe them.

CHAMP: Awww, they adopted it out, I bet.

JOCKEY: Probably sold it.

CYNTHIA: Yeah, I heard of 'em doing that.

EL TORO: I've got my Ma, and a volunteer lawyer trying to track her down. I know in my heart she's alive.

JOCKEY: You saw her alive?

EL TORO: That's how come I know she was a girl. *(She winks at* CHAMP, *beckons her to join in her joke on* JOCKEY—*they both sneak up on* JOCKEY) She was so beautiful . . . when she was born the doctor threw her up on my breast . . . *(directly behind* JOCKEY) . . . and she went right for the nipple! *(They grab* JOCKEY's *breast.)*

JOCKEY: *(shocked, then laughing)* That's a girl all right!

All in shower laugh. MATRON *becomes vaguely aware of the disturbance. She has been totally submerged in her action with* KATHLEEN. EL TORO *immediately acts as if she is comforting* JOCKEY, *who immediately acts as if she's ill.* CHAMP *acts normal, keeps showering as her cover.*

MATRON: All right, keep it down—you're turnin' into prunes.

MATRON *takes* KATHLEEN *from the shower (she was clearly not finished showering) and places her in solitary confinement behind the net.* KATHLEEN *looks for a way out, finds methods of making the time pass during her stay behind "the net." The prisoners finish their showers and dress.* JOCKEY *and* EL TORO *dress, while in line with the others,* JOCKEY *in front of* EL TORO.

JOCKEY: Don't get butch with me—we're not home.

EL TORO: Since when I live at yer house?

JOCKEY: Whatcha got, a hormone rush?

EL TORO: I washed my hands and I can't do a thing with 'em. *(Runs fingers up and down* JOCKEY's *body.)*

JOCKEY: I'll have ta get butch and beat yer ass.

EL TORO: *(Bumping buns)* We could go to different holes together.

JOCKEY: Who ya been takin' butch lessons from?

EL TORO: Not from you, you bum fuck! *(Sticks out tongue)*

JOCKEY: *(Grabs tongue)* You stick that out, ya got to use it.

EL TORO: Why, Miss Butch, you flirting with me?

The violin/bell sounds, women line up for the count. They measure an arm's length between them and begin:

JOCKEY: Six.

RONNIE: Thirteen.

CHAMP: Fifteen.

EL TORO: Twenty-seven.

KATHLEEN: Thirty.

The prisoners move to scrub the floor. As they scrub, RONNIE *transforms into* MATRON 1, CYNTHIA *into* MATRON 2. *They stand back to back—they keep watch. Their eyes dart from prisoner to prisoner, from one audience member to another, checking for disruptions and contraband. They move, still back to back, in a circle as they speak.*

MATRON 1: It's a clear day.

MATRON 2: Not a cloud.

MATRON 1: Did you hear about Lieutenant Meeker?

MATRON 2: What?

MATRON 1: Totaled her car last night.

MATRON 2: Oh, no.

MATRON 1: Yeah, can't save it.

MATRON 2: That car was a classic.

MATRON 1: I always told her if she hung on to it, she'd get five thousand for it in about twenty years.

MATRON 2: I saw an article in *Time* that they're selling old cars down in Austin for fifty to eighty thousand.

MATRON 1: I saw that, too.

MATRON 2: My Dad had a truck come and haul his Oldsmobile away two years ago.

MATRON 1: The one with the fins?

MATRON 2: That's the one.

MATRON 1: How much is it worth now?

MATRON 2: Aw, they squashed it into a cube and sold it for scrap, but if it was in running order, I figure Dad coulda sold it for thirty thousand in about twenty years. There wasn't a dent in it and the chrome was perfect.

MATRON 1: No rust?

MATRON 2: Not that I noticed.

MATRON 1 *plays violin/bell sound. Women line up for count.*

JOCKEY: Seven.

CHAMP: Ten.

EL TORO: Sixteen.

KATHLEEN: Twenty-eight.

MATRON 2: Specified women report to the sewing room . . . *(Going down line at random)* You . . . you . . . you . . . you . . .

If company size allows, MATRON 2 *oversees workers in sewing room. The women who were picked move on to the sewing room where they pantomime folding and ironing sheets. As this happens,* EL TORO *and* JOCKEY *move to the net to tell* KATHLEEN *that they weren't able to get her the contraband (valium) they had promised her. Whispers— discussion ensues. A* MATRON *intervenes. If company is small,* MAT-RON 2 *transforms back into* CYNTHIA *for work in the sewing room.*

MATRON: No talking.

EL TORO: *(Innocent)* Just saying hello.

MATRON: You know the rules.

EL TORO: What's wrong with hello?

MATRON: Nothing. Hello, El Toro. You're elected to scrub this hall. *(Kicks her behind the knee, forcing* EL TORO *to the floor.)*

EL TORO: But I just scrubbed it this morning.

MATRON: It's dirty from all the hellos. Every time you say hello, El Toro, you say it so juicy you get spit on my clean floor. Down on your knees. *(Notices* JOCKEY *still talking quietly to* KATHLEEN*)* You, too. You there.

JOCKEY: Me?

MATRON: You, lady. Down and scrub. *(Hands mop to* JOCKEY, *sponge and bucket to* EL TORO.*)* Learn to be a good little house-keeper and you can get a first-class man when you get out. Real good housekeepers are careful of their work. *(Points out blemishes on floor—*JOCKEY *follows her around and scrubs)* There's a spot, and there's a spot—*(Finds one in front of* EL TORO.*)*

EL TORO: That's your shadow.

MATRON: Why, so it is. *(Kicks bucket, drenching* EL TORO *with water.)* And my shadow just kicked the bucket. Hurry it up, don't let the water get into the cells, or you'll be mopping all week. *(Marching)* Faster, faster. No man would put up with such a slow wife, ladies. Elbow grease, that's what my Grand-dad said it takes—elbow grease.

Gritting their teeth, the two women work as fast as possible to mop up the water.

Scene 5 is the sewing room—circle of light in front of the cells. The prisoners mime folding and ironing sheets and pillowcases. Two MATRONS *are supervising.* MATRON 2 *is the instructor or overseer of the work.* MATRON 1 *has just entered—she stands in front of the net, checks out and collects the tools of the work. This scene is to be done with easy familiarity and playfulness.*

CHAMP: Another day, another two-and-a-half cents from "Sam."

JOCKEY: *(Comes into the sewing room after scrubbing the floor)* Minus two, ya mean.

ALL: Yeah, you can say that again. I know what you mean, etc.

JOCKEY: Yeah, man, when I get out, I'm gonna buy a Silver Cloud Rolls Royce with all the millions I'm earning in this joint.

EL TORO *has come in from scrubbing floors, folds sheets with* JOCKEY.

OX TAIL: You'll be lucky if you can buy one roller skate.

EL TORO: I can't even afford a skate key, I'm so in debt.

OX TAIL: You owe me so many cartons of cigarettes, you'll be the rest of your life paying off.

EL TORO: Ah, c'mon baby, take it out in trade.

OX TAIL: Since ya asked me nice.

CHAMP: *(To* MATRON 1*)* I saw the way you smiled at Mrs. Snowden.

MATRON 1: I'm feeling good today.

JOCKEY: You're always feeling good when you're near Mrs. Snowden.

The others laugh. MATRON 1 *blushes.*

OX TAIL: Hey, look, Mrs. Beecroft is blushing.

MATRON 2: Keep it down to a dull roar. Let's get the work out, okay?

EL TORO: She's sweet on Snowden.

MATRON 1: My husband would be interested to hear that.

CHAMP: What he don't know won't hurt him.

MATRON 1: Okay, cut the kidding.

JOCKEY: Kidding? Who's kidding?

EL TORO: And they put us in the hole for getting married.

MATRON 1: Come on, hurry it up or I'll have to write you up.

JOCKEY: Yer cute when yer mad.

MATRON 2: You listen to too many movies.

OX TAIL: She don't "watch" 'em, that's for sure.

JOCKEY: Would be the waste of a good movie.

CHAMP: Hey, Mrs. Beecroft, can I call you up for a date when I get out of here?

MATRON 1: You'll never get out of here if you spend all your time on love affairs.

CHAMP: Affairs? Affairs? I'm a fine, upstanding, married Christian woman with two children.

OX TAIL: And three wives.

They all laugh.

EL TORO: No, she's only got two. One lucked out of here last week.

MATRON 1: I didn't hear any crying.

CHAMP: This joint is a supermarket and all the tomatoes are free.

OX TAIL: Mrs. Snowden is looking at Mrs. Beecroft, now.

MATRON 2: To signal her to write you up for distracting four people from doing their work. *(She says this with warmth.)*

OX TAIL: Yer an all-right chick, Mrs. Beecroft—

MATRON 1: Woman, not chick.

OX TAIL: That matron on the night shift is some kind of bitch—I mean witch. She makes us obey rules that haven't even been invented yet.

MATRON 1 *crosses to play dissonant chord on violin (the "bell" sound). Prisoners line up for a count.* MATRON 2 *transforms back to* CYNTHIA.

JOCKEY: Three.

CYNTHIA: Eleven.

CHAMP: Fifteen.

OX TAIL: Twenty-two.

EL TORO: Twenty-nine.

KATHLEEN *(From net)*: Thirty-six.

OX TAIL *transforms into* HEAD MATRON. *Other prisoners are still in line.*

MATRON 1: They're bringing in a new load of prisoners.

MATRON 1 *crosses to cell, unlocks door (at O.M.T., rattles chain).* HEAD MATRON *crosses to net, grabs* KATHLEEN, *who transforms into a new prisoner and is walked across the playing area and thrown in cell. The prisoners get very excited as they watch the new ones come in.*

EL TORO: Fresh fish!

JOCKEY: Hot zucchini!

They continue to cat-call and comment on the women: they might have known "that one" from high school or "that one" from a recent local TV show. This banter continues until KATHLEEN *and* MATRON *pass—then* EACH WOMAN *in count line transforms into a* NEW PRISONER *as* KATHLEEN *and* MATRON *pass her. Some of the women may show signs of fatigue and pain from various forms of drug addiction. Others may be jumpy and irritable from heavy drinking. Some may still bear bruises and other marks of their "apprehension" (i.e., forceable arrest). Certain "political prisoners" may be recovering from severe burns on arms, legs, heads or faces (i.e., from being burned out of hideouts by police) or gunshot wounds. Some may be "spaced out" from past heavy drug usage; others may be cool and keep to themselves, or some are easygoing, but show no "heavy" emotion.*

MATRON 1 *transforms into a new arrival and joins the others who are moved en masse by the* HEAD MATRON *across the playing area toward the net. The image the actors project during this move is one of animals being led to slaughter, done in silence, very slowly.*

HEAD MATRON: All right ladies, right this way. *(Takes a prisoner by the arm and leads her to a place behind the net)* Nice to see you so bright this early. *(Sends another prisoner to the net)* Step up to the counter and verify the list of your belongings. *(Leads another prisoner)* This is the last time you'll see them till you get out. *(Takes another prisoner out of line)* If it isn't on the list now, it won't be there when you go home. *(Sends last prisoner to the net)*

All the NEW PRISONERS *are now lined up behind the net. They are captive there.*

EL TORO: *(Intimately, without moving)* I feel like I've known you all my life.

JOCKEY: Me, too.

EL TORO: Who are you?

JOCKEY: A messenger.

EL TORO: What for?

JOCKEY: To make you happy. *(Leans to kiss her.)*

*In the following section two speakers at a time say the same lines, but
with their own rhythms and intentions. In this way, it becomes a jam.*
KATHLEEN *speaks to* EL TORO *across the space between the cells and
the net.* CHAMP *and* CYNTHIA *speak intimately to each other without
moving—they are behind the net.*

KATHLEEN & CHAMP: I need something.

EL TORO & CYNTHIA: I know what you need.

KATHLEEN & CHAMP: How do you know it?

EL TORO & CYNTHIA: Been watching you.

KATHLEEN & CHAMP: I been watching you, too.

EL TORO & CYNTHIA: I want to lay my head down on your
breast.

KATHLEEN & CHAMP: C'mere.

During the following confrontation, the other PRISONERS *behind the
net quietly begin to "look for a way out."* ALL PRISONERS *(including
KATHLEEN in the cell) participate except* RONNIE. *This continues
throughout the scene. The* MATRON *maintains her distance, speaks
from in front of cells toward* RONNIE, *who stands at the side of the net.*

MATRON: What have you got in your hand?

RONNIE: Nothin'.

MATRON: I saw something flash!

RONNIE: Far out. *(Looks around)* Where?

MATRON: Don't be smart. Act like a lady.

RONNIE: If I did you'd arrest me all over again. Ladies are
prostitutes, and I never hooked in my . . .

MATRON: Ladies are ladies, and ladies get respect.

RONNIE: Not where I come from.

MATRON: Hold out your hand or be ready to go before the
disciplinary committee.

RONNIE: *(Reluctantly holds out her hand)* Yes, ma'am.

MATRON: A salt shaker?

RONNIE: Hey, you guessed it.

MATRON: That's enough. (RONNIE *drops imaginary shaker*)
Why'd you take it?

RONNIE: T' brighten up m' room.

MATRON: A salt shaker?

RONNIE: Different strokes for different folks.

MATRON: I'll have to report this.

RONNIE: *(Pleading now, her kidding attitude gone)* Aww, please,
Mrs. Frank, give me a break? I hardly knew I walked out of
the dining room with it—it's just it was shiny, and it's so drab
here.

MATRON: Smarten up! *(Mimes writing something in a little book)*
All right, ladies, you will now line up and strip to your shoes
and socks.

The PRISONERS *come out from behind the net, stand in a straight
line in front of it. As they do,* JOCKEY *unrolls a sheet of white paper
that is attached to two poles and stretches it to the other end of the
platform attaching other pole to metal holders on side of platform,
thus making a scrim that covers the women from neck to mid-thigh.
A light behind the net is turned on and other lights dimmed so the
stripping can be seen in silhouette. The* WOMEN *strip to socks and
shoes.*

MATRON: Hand all your clothes to the inmate who's checked
your belongings list and your clothing will be added to it.
Your new ensemble will be provided by the State.

*Articles of clothing (at O.M.T. the green surgical robes) are passed
down the line toward* JOCKEY, *at far end of line. New clothing (men's
hats and sports jackets) are passed up the line. The* PRISONERS *mime
dressing. They put on sport coats as they would dresses—wiggle into
them, zip . . . they hold hats)*

MATRON: Roll your underwear and other garments up and
hand them to the personnel you see here. Speed it up. We
have to get on to your space assignments.

EL TORO *stands motionless, looking at dress (really a sports jacket, but it's behind white paper). The* HEAD MATRON *addresses her.*

MATRON: What's the matter? Get dressed.

EL TORO: I never wore no dress before.

HEAD MATRON *crosses to lineup, looks under the white paper, crosses away and takes line.*

MATRON: You're a female, I see. That means you'll wear a dress here.

EL TORO: I don't think I can, Ma'am.

MATRON: You'll address me as Lieutenant Meeker.

EL TORO: I can't wear no dress, Lieutenant Meeker.

MATRON: You asking for the hole?

EL TORO: I'm sorry, Lieutenant Meeker, but it will make me sick to wear a dress.

MATRON: You have ten seconds to get it on. *(Looks at watch)* One, two, three, four, five . . .

EL TORO *awkwardly pulls dress (sport coat) on and stands there, mortified.*

MATRON: There now, you look real cute in that. Nobody dies from wearing dresses . . .

EL TORO *faints in place. The other* PRISONERS *catch her, try to revive her.*

MATRON: On your feet. You're holding up the parade. *(Other* PRISONERS *pull* EL TORO *up) (Quieting them down, regaining control)* All right, ladies, you will now pledge allegiance. *(All jump to attention, put their hands to hearts)* We will sing our new, special "Fight Depression" song, so thoughtfully written by our own Miss Schnauzer's grandfather.

The women burst through the paper scrim, wearing men's hats and sports jackets over their dresses. HEAD MATRON *transforms back into* OX TAIL. *She wears sports jacket under guard coat which she removes and joins the others. The subtext of this song is the prisoners' fantasy of themselves as pop-art criminals.*

PRISONERS: *(Sing)* Tighten your belt and
Tough it out.
Some lamebrains born
On the prairies,
Or in the smog-soaked
Basins;
Starved into
Staring awareness,
And suspicious
Short-order cooks
By the Depression—the
"Great Depression" that is—
Have stuffed their faith
Up in holy argyle socks and
Play a loner's game;
Sneaking
On slippery dewy limbs
Fall into spider nets
Saying "I know exactly where I am
At all times.I planned it.
I planned it."

I'm the best damn
Sunday morning quarterback
Who ever lived
And if you doubt it, I'll
Start phoning you long distance
At three (o'clock) in the morning.
My goal-posts are always up
And painted day-glow white.
That's right!
I never sleep
Because I keep
An open eye
On history.
Thirty thousand years from now
I want to see it written—He sold Orange
Julius to the Chinese,
Quadraphonic to the Sudanese,
A *(Insert two-syllable name of local fast food store—i.e., McDonald's*

or Dairy Queen) on every
Kremlin corner.
The Arabs drive Continentals,
And the Shah sleeps peacefully
Steely eyes closed
On a Sealy Posturepedic.
And Chilean-Brazilian generals reside in
Amphibious Cadillacs,
Whose hubcaps are engraved
With the images of doves
Carrying Picasso's eyes
Blazing in their talons.

The Women *peel off their sports coats. The next three lines are said simultaneously as* Kathleen *goes back to her cell,* Ronnie *and the other* Prisoners *go back behind the net.* El Toro *remains in the central playing area.*

El Toro: The first time I tried to kill myself . . .

Ronnie: I tried to kill myself lots of times.

Kathleen: I tried to kill myself three times.

El Toro: *(Alone in the center space—addresses audience)* . . . I waited till everyone was gone to work . . . *(Stops suddenly, looks around, relives fantasy of what it was like to be out on the streets. She feels she is being followed by something. When she is sure she is no longer followed, she continues. This continues throughout the scene in places indicated)* . . . then I got this Japanese carbine that my Dad brought back from the South Pacific . . . *(Stops, looks around, waits, goes on)* . . . and I went into the hall closet with it. *(Takes a breath, looks around, continues)* First I tried to put the barrel of the gun to my temple, but the closet was too small for that. *(Stops, looks, waits, goes on)* So then I remember reading a story in the *Enquirer* about how this guy had blown his head off by putting this shotgun in his mouth—*(Inhales deeply as she says)*—so-o-o-o-o-o-o-o-o-o-, *(Shapes her hand like a psitol, sticks the barrel in her mouth, rotates in a circle with this image so the audience can see, curls up in a ball on the floor)* And I pulled the trigger.

Ronnie: *(From the net)* But I never had enough pills to keep

me out more than twenty-four hours. Except for the time
they kept me in the hole for three months—I lost my mind.

JOCKEY *transforms into* MATRON 3, *puts on guard coat, pushes cart
center, crosses to pull* RONNIE *from behind net and places her in cart.*
EL TORO *continues speaking and moving all around center area.
The cart is solitary confinement, a cell on wheels that is moved up
and down the center space by* MATRON 3. RONNIE *tries desperately
to get out. She scratches messages on the floor with her fingernails,
bangs her head against the bars.*

EL TORO: *(From floor)* It tasted of oil, and
lint . . . *(Rises)* . . . and shit. *(Stops abruptly, looks around, listens, relaxes, goes on)* . . . Then I realized I needed a shell for
the gun, but it was a Jap gun, and none of the shells around
the house would fit it. I got so mad I threw the gun down,
and I decided I'd have to move out since I couldn't find
nothing to use to kill myself. From that day on I was a lot
happier—all I had to do was move out. Why did it take me
so long to find that out?

MATRON 3 *crosses to* KATHLEEN *in cell—she is being prepared for
a medical examination.*

EL TORO: If it's rotten you move—simple as that. Pack up and
move out. *(Joins others behind the net)*

MATRON 3: *(To* KATHLEEN*)* Give me your bra.

KATHLEEN: Watch out, it'll burn ya.

MATRON 3: No talking. One more wisecrack and you go to
the hole. *(*KATHLEEN *opens her mouth, then closes it.)* Shoes,
cigarettes, wristwatch, rings. *(Reaching out from cell to* MATRON
like a balancing act, KATHLEEN *offers some part of her body—leg,
heart, neck—as each item is called for)* Get up on the table and
prepare for your enema. KATHLEEN *looks at her, sneers and
shrugs.)*

RONNIE: *(From solitary where she's been pounding on floor hoping
to find a loose board. She rattles bars—the* MATRONS *who guard her
are expressionless and unhearing. They or* MATRON 3 *turn the cart
in circular fashion in the center area.)* Let me out of here! You
evil bastard bitches—your hair is on fire, and snakes with

blazing fangs live between yer yellow teeth—I seen 'em, I seen 'em. Let me out of here. You hear me! You stinkin' shitheads, ya motherfuckin' dirty daughters of the Jesus lickers—I tell you once and for all, let me out of here! I'll kick this place in and tear you limb from limb, *(Climbs to highest point of cart rail)* and use yer ribs to spear yer hearts, you farts! *(Standing free on top rail)* You can't keep me in here—I won't stay in here!— Don't you know who I am? You let me out of here right now, you sinning, grinning, stuffed-assed satans. *(Jumps down)* Let me out! Right now! I command you! Let me out! *(Continues "Let me out!" as a demand, a plea, beating herself up, etc.)* Let me out! Let me out of here! *(Looks for a way out)*

RONNIE'S *chanting of "Let me out!" incites supportive outcries from the other* WOMEN *behind the net. This becomes a jam of different intentions for the "Let me out!" outcry. It continues through the next three speeches.*

KATHLEEN: *(From the cells—comes right in overlapping "Let me out . . . !")* I really didn't know who I was—I just knew I couldn't take the pain any more. I felt like the sharpest axe was wedged right down my head between my eyes and sinking lower every minute—every single minute the axe was cutting me. It would get to the bottom of my brain, and then another axe would start at the top of my head and slice right down beside the first axe. Not in the same place, but like slicing salami, neat and in a row. The pain of the slicing kept right on. Let me out!

RONNIE: Let me out!

ALL PRISONERS: Let me out!

CYNTHIA: *(Jumps out from behind net to immediately in front of it)* I didn't have no clothes—only a blood-soaked, pissed-out mattress, and a hole in the floor—and it was so cold, the cold ate at my hands and toes as sharp as the axe in my head. *(Lunges and throws herself on cart—*MATRON *shakes her loose.)* I turned into an animal, but smart. *(Mimes picking up spoon from floor, threatens audience.)* I kept a spoon. I told them it had fallen down the shit hole, and I sharpened that spoon—I made that spoon so sharp I could cut my hair with it. Then when it got sharp enough, I lay down on the cold cement floor and I cut both my wrists. Let me out! *(Lies flat on floor)*

RONNIE: Let me out!

KATHLEEN: Let me out!

CHAMP: *(Comes out from behind net to floor)* I can't tell you what a great feeling that was—the pain started to run out of my head, *(Lowers herself onto* CYNTHIA'S *body)* right onto the floor. And I was beginning to relax at last, feeling the pressure just sigh right on out of me. *(Sits up—jam of "Let me out!" stops.)* I'd been waiting and waiting and waiting for that feeling. See—*(Shows the audience a real scar)*—here's the scar. See there?

Each WOMAN *shows one member of the audience a scar she has on her wrist, arm, face, neck, etc. saying:*

EACH PRISONER: See? See there?

ALL WOMEN *enter the solitary cell (the cart). They mime being chained to it by their wrists and pivot in a circle in the center area (at O.M.T.* JOCKEY *pushed with one foot while* OX TAIL *walked it around—she is tethered to the rail of the cart like ox in a yoke.) They testify to the pain of their situation with their hands.*

RONNIE: *(In midst of the others)* But they put me in the hospital and sewed me up. I was so mad they brought me back, I tried to throw things at the nurses. I pulled the tubes out of my arms, but they just kept putting them back. It was so beautiful to die, just like I thought it would be. It was so warm, and my grandmother was waiting for me with her arms out like this—and just as I was going to run into her arms they brought me back. After I healed up they put me back in the hole. I had to eat with my fingers—they wouldn't give me no more spoons.

RONNIE *joins others in testifying with their hands tied to the rail of the cart. The* PRISONERS *sing in harmony.*

PRISONERS: Jesus walked
  This lonesome valley.
He had to walk
  It by himself.

Oh, nobody else
　Could walk it for him.
He had to walk it by himself.

We must walk
　This lonesome valley.
We have to walk
　It by ourselves.
Oh, nobody else
　Can walk it for us.
We have to walk it by ourselves.

They break out of the cart, move to positions across playing area, and taking a vigorous, positive attitude, sing the song as a joyous gospel.

PRISONERS: You "gotta go"
　And stand your trial.
You "gotta go"
　And stand it by yourself.
Oh, nobody else
　Can stand it for you.
You "gotta go" and stand it by yourself.
Yourself!

EL TORO *drops to her knees and begins to scrub toward center of the playing area. From the opposite end of the playing area,* CYNTHIA *scrubs toward her, closer and closer to her. She stares at* EL TORO, *smiles, tries to catch her eye, clears her throat or lets her brush get away from her so that they somehow touch or get very close.*

CYNTHIA: *(Very quietly)* I know who you are. (EL TORO *freezes*) Don't worry. Lotsa people love you. (EL TORO *slowly but deliberately scrubs away from her*) Really, don't worry. I'm not gonna blow yer cover.

In a rage, JOCKEY *charges across the floor.*

JOCKEY: *(Points roughly at* CYNTHIA*)* I'm gonna get you—*(To two other* PRISONERS *walking across the space)* and then I'm gonna get *you*—and then *(To* EL TORO*)* I'm gonna get *you*.

CYNTHIA: *(Stands between* JOCKEY *and* EL TORO*)* Oh now yer not, because first ya gotta go through *me*.

JOCKEY *shoves* CYNTHIA *away, grabs* EL TORO *by the collar and starts to knock her around*—EL TORO *starts to laugh.*

EL TORO: Keep it up and one day you might connect.

JOCKEY: *(Frustrated)* You told Betsie you were going to take Dana away from me.

EL TORO: Nobody can take anyone unless they're ready to go.

JOCKEY: *(Lunges at* EL TORO*)* You bitch!

EL TORO: *(Freeing herself)* Butch—that's *butch.*

CYNTHIA: *(Cracking up)* Ya don't wanna get all messed . . .

JOCKEY: I'm gonna fix yer mouth so's you won't be able to ever eat again, let alone kiss anyone. *(Lunges at* EL TORO*)*

EL TORO: *(Playing with* JOCKEY*)* Keep holding my collar just like that. *(They dance together.)* Yes, that's it, a perfect tilt to the chin and a one and a two and a . . .

EL TORO *lets* JOCKEY *have it. On the way down,* JOCKEY *snatches* EL TORO*'s glasses and smashes them.*

JOCKEY: *(Threatening)* I'll put out yer eyes, you creep, you twerp. You can't move in on me.

EL TORO: *(Standing ground)* Give me back my glasses, you motherfucker, or I'll sit on your rotten guts till they burst that yellow shit out all over our nice clean floor.

CYNTHIA: *(Taking* EL TORO *by the hand)* Let's get the fuck outa here.

EL TORO: *(Resisting)* I want her head—I'm gonna blast it open. She's got my glasses.

JOCKEY, EL TORO *and* CYNTHIA *run out.*

RONNIE: *(She's been keeping watch from cell)* Run. We'll get it. Come on.

In the cells KATHLEEN, RONNIE *(whose "code" name is* GARY*),* CHAMP *and* JOCKEY *are talking.* KATHLEEN *and* RONNIE *are in one cell,* CHAMP *and* JOCKEY *in another. The rest of the women transform into other* PRISONERS. *The transformation is seen through*

*changes in their walks as they move through the yard, to the warden's
office, or back to their cells. With each new walk, the* PRISONERS *give
themselves a new destination.*

KATHLEEN: What's wrong?

GARY: Nothin'.

KATHLEEN: *(Hugging her)* What you mean, nothin'? Tears
streaming down your face all morning.

CHAMP: She's always blue about something.

GARY: *(Shaking* KATHLEEN *off)* It's my anniversary.

CHAMP: Why, you should be happy.

KATHLEEN: Yeah—I don't have anniversaries. I wish I had an
anniversary. I done broke up with everyone!

GARY: Not mine you wouldn't.

JOCKEY: *(To* CHAMP*)* It's the anniversary of her coming out of
the closet.

CHAMP: Yeah, you can still see the splinters in her fists, where
she was pounding on the door.

JOCKEY *and* CHAMP *hit each other and laugh and laugh.*

GARY: You two are so tough, you miss out on really feeling
anything.

KATHLEEN: *(Approaching gently)* Aw, don't mind them—they
just like to show off. *(Embracing her)* Are you in love, honey.

GARY: Oh yes. I love a strong man. He stood up to the whole
world. He taught me how to take it. I can do easy time because
of him. I know I'm going to see him again. Today's our
anniversary. Two weeks ago the pigs shot him.

KATHLEEN: *(Holding* GARY*)* Oh honey, I'm so sorry.

CHAMP: *(To* KATHLEEN*)* You gonna fall for that?

JOCKEY: *(To* CHAMP*)* Kick it off—don't hurt her more. You're
as bad as the pigs.

CHAMP: *(Pulling up her fist and threatening* JOCKEY*)* Take that back.

JOCKEY: Simmer down.

CHAMP *and* JOCKEY *wrestle in cell.*

GARY: *(At* CHAMP *and* JOCKEY*)* You *are* as bad as the pigs. Fight and shoot, shoot and fight.

CHAMP: *(Pinning* JOCKEY *to the floor)* You're lying.

GARY: It's my anniversary.

CHAMP: Anniversary of your biggest lie.

GARY: I'm not lying.

CHAMP: *(Get up, moves to bars)* Yea, you are. When I got here you told me your name was Tania.

GARY: Shut up.

CHAMP: You name isn't Tania, is it?

GARY: That was one of my names. But you're not to say it out loud.

CHAMP: You want to know her new code name? It's Gary. Who ever heard of a femme calling herself Gary Gilmore.

KATHLEEN, *who has continued to try to comfort* GARY, *backs off.*

GARY: *(No longer looking at* CHAMP*)* I'm calling you crazy. No one would do that.

CHAMP: *(To others)* She told me in the shower her new name was Gary.

GARY: They shot him. He wanted me to go with him.

CHAMP: Tell the others you made it up.

GARY: You're too coarse to understand. It's between his spirit and mine.

CHAMP: There ain't nothin' between you and him but six feet of dirt.

GARY: He lives through me.

CHAMP: He was shot at sunrise.

GARY: I took his name to keep him alive.

CHAMP: *(Swings out of her cell, struts across yard)* Don't you wish you'd met him, baby. You never met a bad-ass like that. The most you ever had was a toothless Hell's Angel who stole you away from your Granddaddy's trailer camp. *(Turns to* RONNIE / GARY *and mocks her.)* He shoved his tongue in your ear when he stole you away and you fell madly in love with his gun and his bike—ain't that right?

RONNIE / GARY *jumps from her cell and goes after* CHAMP.

GARY: You bitch!

CHAMP: *(Trying to hold her off)* See what I mean. Holier Than Thou! Look at this wildcat.

GARY: I'm him and he's me, now.

CHAMP: Next thing you'll be Claudine Longet and Tokyo Rose.

GARY: They pardoned her, you dope.

CHAMP: You're the dope, you doped-out nut.

GARY: *(Pulling self away)* You're so square you don't know nothing—you're only Champ. I can be as many people as I want to be.

CHAMP: *(To audience and other* PRISONERS*)* See what I mean. She makes her life up out of the TV news.

GARY: *(Lunges at her)* You make your life up out of comic books.

CHAMP: There's a difference?

They fight fiercely, rolling around on the floor, scratching and kicking. The OTHER PRISONERS *stop and watch, cheer for one or the other, or keep walking so as not to get involved.*

GARY: *(During the fight)* I'm in love. I'm in love with the whole world.

They continue to fight ferociously. The WARDEN'S *voice comes over the loudspeaker.*

WARDEN: Ladies!

RONNIE *and* CHAMP *and all* PRISONERS *freeze, look toward voice and listen.*

WARDEN: Ladies!

RONNIE *and* CHAMP *separate as if nothing had been going on.*

WARDEN: Please proceed to your cells.

PRISONERS *run to the cells from wherever they are. They move from cell to cell, cleaning, stashing contraband. Twinkle lights flash as the* WARDEN *continues.*

WARDEN: Dress appropriately for Sunday worship. Today we will be graced by a visit from the Pentecostal Church. Cells must be cleaned and left in pristine condition as if the Legislature were visiting us. Remember, you are Christian Ladies who keep your houses Christian clean. Your room and your person are reflections of what is going on inside. If you have a messy room or present a messy person, what can anyone think but that your head is a mess . . . (PRISONERS *run to area in front of net, put on "Ladies" hats and transform into members of the Pentecostal Church*) . . . and therefore, a perfect workshop for the Devil? Ladies, give thought to cleanliness, dress in your Sunday best, and then proceed to the chapel. Give our visitors your undivided attention. They've come a long way to bring us Good News.

The area in front of net is suddenly bathed in bright light. The piano, accordion or violin begins to play church chords. The Pentecostal CHURCH MEMBERS *are huddled together, terrified of the* PRISONERS. RONNIE *has transformed into the* HEAD WOMAN *who gives the others strength and sends them into the jail to spread the good word as she speaks.*

HEAD WOMAN: *(Church chords continue under her speech)* You are in the funhouse . . . (*She holds* OX TAIL, *one of the parishioners, who goes bravely into the prison*) . . . of the Lord. (*Touches two more women,* EL TORO *and* CYNTHIA, *who receive strength and go forth bravely*) But be very careful . . . (*Gives strength to another woman,* JOCKEY, *who moves onto the floor*) . . . that you do not make fun of the Holy Ghost. (*Holds* CHAMP *and sends her off.*)

The PENTECOSTALS *are gathered together in the center playing area.*
They are less terrified after being reassured by the HEAD WOMAN,
but they still hold onto one another while reaching out to the PRISONERS
(at O.M.T. the audience became the PRISONERS *in the actors' minds*
at this point) to spread the faith for their salvation.

ALL PARISHIONERS: *(Sing)*
Even if you don't know how to pray
The ghost within you does.
Listen
Listen
Listen
Listen.
Let the maimed ape have her say.
Let your English mind
Get lost, go blind—;
Take the plunge and speak in tongues.

Mother song
And father sound,
Take the plunge
And speak in tongues.
Listen
Listen
Listen.

During the second verse of "Speak in Tongues," CYNTHIA *and*
RONNIE *as* PARISHIONERS *come together center. They are excited.*
OX TAIL *and* EL TORO *continue to sing and preach—they have*
clearly taken the role of Pentecostal ministers. The MINISTERS *sense*
the new excitement—they direct their energies to CYNTHIA *and* RON-
NIE, *who separate and begin to look inward.*

JOCKEY, KATHLEEN, EL TORO, & CHAMP: *(Sing as* PARISHION-
ERS)
Even if you don't know how to pray
The ghost within you does.

OX TAIL: *(As* MINISTER *directs energy toward* RONNIE)
Listen
Listen
Listen

(OX TAIL *touches* RONNIE)
Let the maimed ape have . . .

RONNIE *screams, possessed, falls to floor and is caught by* JOCKEY.
*She begins to speak in tongues. She raises, still speaking in tongues
and moves in a rhythmic dance.*

OX TAIL: . . . her say.

EL TORO: *(As* MINISTER *directs energy toward* CYNTHIA)
Take the plunge . . .

CYNTHIA *screams, possessed, falls and is caught by* KATHLEEN. *She
begins to speak in tongues, rises and moves in a rhythmic dance.*

. . . and speak in tongues.
Mother song
And father sound.

As the song "Speak in Tongues comes to an end, OTHER MEMBERS
*of the group become obsessed, fall to the floor and speak in tongues.
As the speaking goes on, they let their tongues direct the movements
of their bodies until they are lifted off the floor and go into rhythmic
dance.* PARISHIONERS *who speak in tongues during the song keep
the volume down, allowing it to rise when the* SINGERS *are silent.*

KATHLEEN *and* JOCKEY *(still as* PARISHONERS) *scream, possessed.
Then they begin to speak in tongues and rhythmically move in dance.
With* PARISHONERS *speaking in tongues,* OX TAIL *as* MINISTER
1 *and* EL TORO *as* MINISTER 2 *come to the center and pray.*

MINISTER 1: I pray to the Lord with all my heart and soul to
give me the grace and understanding to interpret the messages
you are sending here. Especially for all the souls gathered
here today in your name. Hallelujah, praise the Lord. The
Power is moving. The Power is speaking.

She is drawn to CYNTHIA, *who is speaking in tongues, and lays her
hands on her.*

MINISTER 1: Praise the Lord. Hallelujah. This sweet soul is
saying . . . (CYNTHIA *becomes silent as her speaking in tongues is
translated by the* MINISTER) "Bask in the light and believe, sisters,
and believe, brothers. The Lord is here—we are blessed and

loved if we will only open up our hearts." Do you believe? I believe! Praise the Lord!

CYNTHIA *continues to move rhythmically in celebration. She no longer speaks in tongues.*

MINISTER 2: Praise the Lord! (*Moves to* RONNIE *who is speaking in tongues, lays hands on her*) And this dear child of God, this believer is saying to us brothers and sisters . . . What? (*Pulls "Tongues" speech from* RONNIE *and translates—*RONNIE *is silenced*) . . . "This container is too small . . . " (*Puzzles over this for a moment, then bows head, smiles and looks up*) Thank you, Lord.

RONNIE: (*Dancing rhythmically in celebration*) Thank you, Jesus.

MINISTER 1: Praise the Lord, Hallelujah! God is sending me the ability to translate this divine message into English.

MINISTER 2: The message is coming now, through this instrument who speaks in tongues—

MINISTER 1: —this instrument created in God's image.

MINISTERS 1 *and* 2 *lay hands on* KATHLEEN *and* JOCKEY *who are still speaking in tongues. Looking up into the light, they begin to translate—at first haltingly, then building with full confidence.* JOCKEY *and* KATHLEEN *stop speaking as their tongues are translated.*

MINISTER 2: The answer to the question, "Where are the women inventors and artists of the past?" is . . .

The MINISTERS *move to the center of the playing area, stand back to back and move in a circle. Each revelation comes to them like a bolt of lightning.*

MINISTER 1: They were in the kitchen inventing corn bread.

MINISTER 2: They were in the kitchen inventing chili.

MINISTER 1: They were in the kitchen inventing granola.

MINISTER 2: They were in the kitchen inventing salad.

MINISTER 1: They were in the kitchen inventing meatloaf.

MINISTER 2: They were in the kitchen inventing egg foo young.

MINISTER 1: They were in the kitchen inventing knishes.

MINISTER 2: They were in the kitchen inventing the hot dog.

MINISTER 1: They were in the kitchen inventing spaghetti.

MINISTER 2: They were in the kitchen inventing pancakes.

MINISTER 1: They were in the kitchen inventing butter.

MINISTER 2: They were in the kitchen inventing fire.

MINISTER 1: They were in the bedroom inventing quilts.

MINISTER 2: They were in the bathroom inventing perfume.

MINISTER 1: They were in the bathroom inventing soap.

MINISTER 2: They were in the bathroom inventing the bath.

MINISTER 1: They were in the sewing room inventing clothes.

MINISTER 2: They were in the earth inventing farming.

MINISTER 1: They were in the woods inventing dancing.

MINISTER 1: They were by the waterfall inventing singing.

Both MINISTERS *remove their hats.*

MINISTER 1: (*As* OX TAIL, *her prisoner self*) They were in your arms—inventing loving.

All PARISHIONERS *take off their hats. A very, very brief smile to audience. Then all run to the television room area in front of cells and sit down to watch TV. Throughout this scene they rearrange and knock each other around to get the best view of the TV.* KATHLEEN *is in her cell, separated from the rest, but also watches the TV.*

CHAMP: I'm sick of *Sesame Street!*

EL TORO: The Warden loves it.

KATHLEEN: Change the channel.

JOCKEY: I wanna see . . .

RONNIE: (*Covering* JOCKEY'S *mouth*) Close your mouth and maybe you can.

JOCKEY: Your mother sucks worms.

RONNIE: That's what yer Daddy's got fer a dick.

JOCKEY: I'm gonna tie you to the wall and you got to watch *Sesame Street* forever.

RONNIE: I'd rather watch that than your ugly mug.

CHAMP: Be cool. Be cool.

EL TORO: Mrs. Johnson's gonna put you in the hole.

RONNIE: Where you was born.

JOCKEY: Right behind you. You was born out of a behind.

RONNIE: Shithead.

JOCKEY: You look like the garbage can on the TV show.

RONNIE: Lame, you're too dumb to fight with.

JOCKEY: I get my ideas from the cookie monster.

KATHLEEN: The Munsters have returned.

EL TORO: Morticia, let's start burning the bodies.

CHAMP: Here, light 'em with vampire piss—it works faster than lighter fluid.

KATHLEEN: Shut up, all of you—I'm trying to learn to spell.

RONNIE: The hell with you. (*Singing*) "Take me away baby, baby. Come closer to me and I'll give you my secret key."

CHAMP: Turn up the show and drown out that cat in heat.

CYNTHIA *and* EL TORO *transform into* MATRON 1 *and* MATRON 2. *They put on coats by the cells and walk toward the Warden's area, keeping a careful eye on members of the audience, nodding at someone they know, looking for contraband, stopping any trouble they see. When they reach the net, they keep watch, then do the following as a "conductor" exercise.*

MATRON 1: (*As they watch* OX TAIL) She's so cool all the time.

MATRON 2: Is she real or acting?

MATRON 1: Anyone who winds up here and acts as sweet as that has got to be acting?

MATRON 2: She'll do easy time then.

MATRON 1: Not if I get to her.

MATRON 2: You're taking this job too serious.

MATRON 1: What else is there to do? God put me on this earth for a reason. I'm a good wife. I try and pray to be a good mother, and if I can help one other person, then my life will be worthwhile.

MATRON 2: She's so sweet. Are you sure it's an act?

MATRON 1: The Warden said if we can get her angry and fighting, then sure as shootin' we can "get through" and help her straighten out.

MATRON 2: But it takes so much energy to deal with them when they fight back.

MATRON 1: You're a Christian, aren't you?

MATRON 2: Of course I'm a Christian!

MATRON 1: Then take pity on that poor girl, and do what you have to do to get her to see the light.

MATRON 2: I admire you—I really, really do. I try hard to be a good Christian, but I'm not clear all the time in my mind, just what's the right way to go about . . .

MATRON 1: I never have any doubt about what is right and what is wrong. I never have had—my Daddy and Mama taught me that real early.

They take one last look at the yard, then march back to the cells, keeping their eyes on both sides of the audience as they go. MATRON 2 *transforms back into* EL TORO. CYNTHIA *remains* MATRON 1 *and rattles chain on cells, signaling the women to come down into the yard for recreation.* PRISONERS *wear gym shorts and "Coyote" (the prostitutes' union) t-shirts. Some are doing calisthenics, some play basketball, jump rope, run in place, etc. Cell lights and twinkle lights come up abruptly on* RONNIE'S *cell.*

RONNIE: (*Very "spaced out"*) I got busted last summer in Colorado Springs. What a lousy jail. All we got to eat twice a day was cold oatmeal, nothin' to put on it, and coffee made o' sewer water. They gave us Top tobacco to smoke. Stale—it was so stale, I like to set my eyebrows on fire ev'r' time I lit up. *Whoooooooosh* like the Fourth o' July. Went to the hospital with second-degree burns on my eyelids. No shit. No shit! They finally felt so bad about it they let me out for only six bucks. So I high-tailed it for Boulder. There I spent three beautiful days with the spaced-out dude in a bare van. There was nothing in this big Dodge van but, get this, man—nothing in it but this giant black leather rocking chair. This spaced-out dude, he had this chair built just for him for tripping. He loved that chair so much he took it on vacation with him. Hooked this fucking chair right up to the generator, and man, he'd sit in it, drop PCP, MBD, acid, and half my thorazines, and he'd rock himself into ecstatic oblivion. You know what he had built into the seat of his chair?—vibrator, man. *(Pause)* Far out!

Lights come down on RONNIE, *up on* EL TORO, *who stands behind the net—she is high on pills.*

EL TORO: Hi, my name's Toro. Man, I'm clean, no shit. Wanna see my arms? Look. *(Rolls up sleeves)* See there— you can't see no tracks there. I quit the needle. I quit it. I quit the needle and I cut my hair. See how clean and neat I look, just like they want me. Never found me real mother till I was sixteen. Ain't that right, Champ?

CHAMP: *(Doing calisthenics in the yard)* That's right, Toro.

EL TORO: This here is my friend Champ. We was together in reform school. We was there four or five years. Hell, Champ was born there—right, Champ? We been in forever. We know the score—right, Champ?

CHAMP: Right.

EL TORO: *(Rolls up sleeves again)* See them arms? When I first kissed my husband I fell right in love with him. Just like that, my knees went just like this. *(Wiggles knees, "makes like" to faint)* I went home and told my Mom—I hadn't known my Mom too long at the time—it took me so fuckin' long to find her—but I told her, I'm gonna marry that guy, and sure enough, four weeks later we was married, and four weeks after that I started on the needle. But then he ratted on me, so I shot him. You seen the bullet holes, didn't you Champ?

CHAMP: I seen 'em, Toro.

After her speech, RONNIE *comes down from her cell, puts on a guard coat and transforms into a* MATRON. *She doesn't hear* EL TORO, *who's in another part of the building. She signals to other prisoners that recreation is over and they must scrub the floor. She throws scrub brushes to them.*

EL TORO: Sure enough. But we got lucky and we're still in love. Then we got busted together for dealing—he's in prison at the men's penal complex.

CHAMP: The penis complex.

EL TORO: Right, that's what *I* got. Anyway, we got lucky and we're still in love, he didn't die, but what a rat he was. Well, I can't help it—I did fall in love with him, just like lightning striking . . . that's the way it was.

Lights come down on EL TORO. *Focus shifts to the floor where the* PRISONERS *are scrubbing, covering sections of the floor in pairs:* OX TAIL *and* CHAMP, CYNTHIA *and* EL TORO *(who has come down and joined her),* JOCKEY *and* KATHLEEN.

MATRON: *(Talks down to prisoners)* You ladies should be down like that on your knees three times a day, thanking the good Lord you were born in this time, in this country.

MATRON'S *attention shifts, with crowlike eyes, to the audience—eyes darting from one person to another each time the* PRISONERS *sing.* PRISONERS *sing to each other, then tenderly caress, cuddle and make love to each other, always keeping an eye on the matron to be sure that her eyes are elsewhere. When the* MATRON *speaks, the* WOMEN *begin furiously scrubbing.*

OX TAIL: *(Sings to* CHAMP*)*
You may put your head down,
You may sink into the pillows of love.

JOCKEY: *(Sings to* KATHLEEN*)*
You may put your hand down,

You may unclench the fist,
You may unlock your joints.

PRISONERS *separate and go back to fierce scrubbing when they hear the* MATRON *say:*

MATRON: Before this great country was made into a country, you, Jockey, you, Ox Tail, and you, Champ, would 'a been hanged. Just like that. No if 's and's or but's. Taken out and hanged by your neck until you were dead . . . for stealing, for picking pockets. No pleading, no mercy— out! Hanged!

MATRON *changes focus to the audience, looking for contraband, sudden movements, anything suspicious.* PRISONERS *sing and tenderly caress one another,* MATRON *still oblivious.*

CYNTHIA: (*Sings to* EL TORO)
You may put your head down,
You my sink into the pillows of love.

KATHLEEN: (*Sings to* JOCKEY)
EL TORO: (*Sings to* CYNTHIA)
CHAMP: (*Sings to* OX TAIL)
You may put your belly down.
The Lord will provide.
There is no need to strive
For food or drink.

MATRON: (PRISONERS *separate and scrub*) For a misdemeanor they'd cut off your hands. For adultery, a brand on your forehead—a big brand right here in the middle of your forehead—and without a valium yet.

PRISONERS *join hands, dance in a circle around the* MATRON, *who doesn't see them because she's watching the audience.*

PRISONERS: (*Sing*) Music will fill
All the empty spaces.
You may lay away need,
Dissolve desire.

They spin out, re-form with same partners, go to three separate areas of the floor.

OX TAIL, JOCKEY & CYNTHIA: (*Sing*)
Stay a while.

CHAMP, KATHLEEN & EL TORO: (*Sing*)
Stay a while.

KATHLEEN & JOCKEY: (*Sing in center section*)
Hello eye—may I have the next dance?
Hello lips—be still now.

PRISONERS *scrub.*

MATRON: You don't know how lucky you are, ladies. How'd you like that, El Toro—get those pretty hands of yours cut off, for bad checks—both of them? How'd you like that?

JOCKEY: *I'd like it,* because then I'd be done with you! (MATRON *turns quickly, signals her to get back to work*)

EL TORO: (*Sings*) Your heart beats out our trance.

CHAMP: (*Sings*)
Hello tongue—this trip has just begun.

ALL PRISONERS & MATRON: (*Sing*)
This is the place
Where light is feed.
The Lord will provide.
I've got what you need.
You may hide your sweet, burdened head
In this dancing bed.

The PRISONERS *continue scrubbing.* EL TORO *quickly and cautiously scrubs toward* JOCKEY, *stares at her, smiles, tries to catch her eye, clears her throat, or lets her brush get away from her so that they somehow touch or get very close.*

EL TORO: (*Very quietly*) I know who you are. (JOCKEY *freezes*) Don't worry. Lotsa people love you . . . (JOCKEY *deliberately scrubs away from her*) Really, don't worry. I'm not gonna blow yer cover.

They freeze. Lights come down slowly.

END OF ACT ONE

Act Two

More new women prisoners are being admitted. They enter in darkness and take their places behind the net. As the lights come up, they project images of "looking for a way out". The group stops and listens, moves together, stops together. They range in age from 17 to 60. Those who've never been to prison before might keep their eyes downcast (they try to minimize their presence). The political prisoners hold themselves erect and proud. They size up the situation and try to make contact with those with whom they can establish "lines" of sympathy. "Repeaters" are greeted like alums returning to an old school, by both inmates and guards with hearty recognition. CHAMP is not among the prisoners—she enters the yard as MATRON.

MATRON: Take a chair, ladies. When your name is called, come forward to claim your property and valuables—and, I repeat—check the list. Bessie Mayo.

KATHLEEN (*Transformed into* BETSY) That's Betsy!

MATRON: The name on the official Deparment list is Bessie, so that's your name.

BETSY: They wrote it down wrong.

MATRON: (*Flat tone, calling out again*) Bessie Mayo.

BETSY: My name is Betsy. I won't be called a name not my own.

MATRON: You are in prison. You have no more rights. You gave up your rights when you committed the crime that sent you here. The name on my list, written here by the Authorities, is Bessie Mayo.

BETSY: Betsy!

MATRON: Any more outbursts and you'll be taken to Adjustment.

EL TORO: Shut up, honey, and do like she says, or they throw you in the hole.

BETSY: I protest this deliberate dehumanizing process. You are beginning by taking way my own name. Well, it's going to stop right here, because I will not tolerate . . .

MATRON: Oh, swell, we got a Commie in this bunch. Take her away.

BETSY *backs away from the net. The following roll call may be added to or changed at any given performance to include some names of audience members or newsworthy people. The actors transform to these different personalities. We used a set order in which the actors always responded: (1)* EL TORO *(2)* JOCKEY *(3)* RONNIE, *etc.*

MATRON: Adelle Novas.

ADELLE: Here.

MATRON: Marijane Scoppetone.

MARIJANE: Here.

MATRON: Maimie Eisenhower.

MAIMIE: Here.

MATRON: Ida Lupino.

IDA: Here.

MATRON: Happy Ford.

HAPPY: Here.

PRISONERS *begin to come out from behind the net and line up in front of it.*

MATRON: Betty Rockefeller.

BETTY: Here.

MATRON: Louise Lasser.

LOUISE: Here.

MATRON: Tricia DietRite.

TRICIA: Here.

MATRON: Amy Carter.

AMY: Here.

MATRON: Marlena Dexadrine.

MARLENE: Here.

MATRON *crosses to net, turns, removes her jacket and becomes a* PRISONER. *She joins the others, who are acting out their fantasies of what they'll do and be when they get out. They dream of being safe-crackers, tennis champs, typists, etc.*

JOCKEY: (*Sings, as others continue acting out their fantasies*)
When I get out of here
I'm gonna make so much money
I'll never have any fear. (*Runs onto floor and sits*)

RONNIE: (*Sings*) When I get out of here (*Punches others, who fall like dominoes*) I'm gonna dress so sharp (*Jives on floor*) And keep my eyes piercing clear.

OX TAIL *and* CYNTHIA *pick up* JOCKEY, EL TORO *picks up* RON-NIE, *both groups perform flying images.* CHAMP *and* KATHLEEN *perform images singly.*

I'll buy me a Lear jet
And you can bet—

ALL: I'm gonna fly, I'm gonna fly.

RONNIE: I'm gonna go go go go go go go go go go! (*Flying image ends*)

KATHLEEN: (*Sings, with others keeping time from floor*)
When I get out of here
I'll get me so much bread
They'll think I invented dough

ALL: (*Sing*) I'll jet by so high you won't see me go,
I'll jet by so high you won't see me go,
I'll jet by so high you won't see me go!
I'll be so high,
I'll be so high,
You won't see me go go go go go go go go go go!

JOCKEY, OX TAIL *and* KATHLEEN *transform into* MATRON 1,

MATRON 2 *and* MATRON 3. MATRON 1 *begins to harass a* PRISONER *and push her around for no visible reason. (She may not have scrubbed floor properly, or she may have been seen "with" another prisoner.)* MATRONS 2 *and* 3 *intervene causing* MATRON 1 *to let* PRISONER *go, then they bring* MATRON 1 *with them to the* WARDEN'S *area where all three keep watch on the yard.*

MATRON 1: I did what I had to do.

MATRON 2: You kept control.

MATRON 3: Best of all, you kept control of *yourself.*

MATRON 1: I'm a human being—I have feelings just like anybody else.

MATRON 2: You did right.

MATRON 3: Every time something like that's happened, it's always from nerves.

MATRON 2: It's usually always nerves.

MATRON 3: These girls all got too many nerves. 'member one from Birmingham, was wound up all the time? Her eyes just glowed.

MATRON 2: I remember her—all the girls had crushes on her.

MATRON 3: Like to scratch each other's eyes out.

MATRON 2: They was always searching her cell and her body.

MATRON 3: The Warden was sure she was on something.

MATRON 2: It was just nerves, just nerves that made her eyes glow like that—but let me tell you, no one wanted to turn their backs on her.

MATRON 1: Should I call?

MATRON 2: Honey, it isn't your fault. She'll pull through.

MATRON 1: I swear I thought she'd stuffed a pillow in her stomach, just to bug me. It didn't look natural the way her belly was spread out like that. She was flat as a board at morning count.

MATRON 3: Some of these women is just demons—they can

think their way into anything. She got herself all worked up just because her mother died. She'll be okay in the morning, mark my words.

MATRON 1: I didn't hit her. I'm not the type. I'd never lose control like that.

During the following "nodding" lines, the actors continue the nodding action as an "emblem" throughout the speech.

MATRON 2: I was there. You just pushed on her belly to see if it was a pillow.

MATRON 1: (*Nods*) That's right. That's all I did.

MATRON 3: (*Nods*) I can just hear the troublemakers now.

MATRON 1: (*Nods*) That Squaw was standing just round the corner. She's telling the whole population I hit her in the stomach and that's why she swelled up. (*Nodding stops*)

MATRON 3: In the old days they'd have thrown her in the hole til she got over agitating. They kept an Indian in there once til she went blind— didn't give nobody any trouble after that, you can bet your boots.

MATRON 1: It's not my fault they won't give her leave to go to the funeral. I don't make the rules.

MATRON 2: Just grief made her belly act like that. My God, she looked eight months pregnant.

MATRON 3: She was flat as a board this morning.

MATRON 2: It's just nerves, honey. You did your job, and you kept yourself in control in front of the rest of them. That's what you're supposed to do and that's what you're paid to do.

MATRON 1: If we took them in our arms every time they got bad news from home, the whole place would fall apart.

MATRON 3: You can bet your boots.

MATRON 2: You can say that again.

They stand at attention, remove their uniform jackets and transform back into PRISONERS.

All PRISONERS *now "walk" back and forth from the net to their cells. Some interact non-verbally asking for tenderness, others maintain solitude, some look for comfort, a fight, etc. Those they "ask" comply or resist, but some sort of contact is made. This contact is always broken when they hear something, think a guard is approaching or are "caught in the act" and each continues walking alone until a new contact is made. The walking continues until* RONNIE *and* EL TORO *are in their cells—then the others move quickly to theirs.* CHAMP *and* KATHLEEN *share the same cell.* CHAMP *rubs* KATHLEEN'S *back.*

EL TORO: (*To* RONNIE *who's transformed into an older woman*) What are you in for?

RONNIE: (*As older woman*) Life.

EL TORO: I mean . . . charge . . . ?

RONNIE: (*Looks at her a moment*) Oh yeah . . . murder.

They freeze. So do OX TAIL, JOCKEY *and* CYNTHIA *who've been listening. Focus shifts to* KATHLEEN *and* CHAMP.

CHAMP: What are you in for?

KATHLEEN: Bum rap.

CHAMP: Aren't we all?

KATHLEEN: I didn't do anything.

CHAMP: But they caught you at it.

KATHLEEN: I was in the wrong place . . .

CHAMP: . . . at the wrong time . . .

KATHLEEN: Yeah . . .

They freeze. Focus shifts to RONNIE, EL TORO *and* JOCKEY.

EL TORO: Wow.

JOCKEY: When.

RONNIE: When what?

OX TAIL: When'd ya do it?

RONNIE: Many lives ago.

JOCKEY: Who was it?

RONNIE: A husband of that period.

OX TAIL: Did you do it?

RONNIE: I didn't, but it doesn't matter. I did it a lot in my head, before and since.

They freeze. Focus shifts to KATHLEEN *and* CHAMP.

CHAMP: I been watching you.

KATHLEEN: Oh?

CHAMP: Been watching you eat.

KATHLEEN: Yeah?

CHAMP: I like to watch your mouth. (KATHLEEN *laughs.* CHAMP *stops rubbing*) You got family?

KATHLEEN: I guess.

CHAMP: (*Pushes her*) Do ya or don't ya?

KATHLEEN: (*Confused*) They're still there, I guess.

CHAMP: (*Starts to get rougher*) Where?

KATHLEEN: (*Moves away*) South Dakota.

CHAMP: (*Shakes* KATHLEEN) How long since you were home?

KATHLEEN: (*Presses herself*) Left at fifteen.

CHAMP: (*Pins her up against wall*) Didn't they try to stop you?

KATHLEEN: (*Stands up to* CHAMP) I didn't give 'em a chance. I ironed all my Dad's shirts and I left.

CHAMP: (*This was the response she wanted—it was a game*) Far out . . . I really like the look of you.

KATHLEEN: (*Still confused*) Thanks.

They freeze. Focus shifts to RONNIE *and the others.*

EL TORO: How long you been in the joint?

RONNIE: Sixteen years here. Four in the maximum facility.

Eighteen months before that in the county jail. That was the pits. The others were better, but (*Reaches over to stroke* JOCKEY) this one's best of all.

JOCKEY: But you shoulda been paroled by now.

RONNIE: They've been trying to get me out of here all right.

OX TAIL: Were you given a fair hearing?

RONNIE: They granted parole, three times now, but I refused it.

EL TORO: Why? Why? Why? I . . . I want outa here so bad I . . .

RONNIE: I'm innocent.

JOCKEY: No shit.

RONNIE: Besides, it's safer here than on the streets or even in my own home.

JOCKEY: But it's so boring.

All fall into images of enormous boredom for a beat. They change into other images of boredom in time with the musical introduction. They leave their cells and create one big "bored" image in front of the cells. Their action during this "scat" song is to find relief from the boredom of prison—they act out fantasies of what they'd like to do if free. They start in front of the cells and move, singing and dancing, across the whole yard.

EL TORO, CHAMP & OX TAIL (*Sing*)	JOCKEY & KATHLEEN (*Sing*)	RONNIE (*Sings*)
I'm bored		
	I'm bored	
		I'm bored
I'm sick		
And tired		
I'm sick and		
Tired		
Of being		
Sick		
And tired.		
I'm sick and		

EL TORO, CHAMP & OX TAIL (*Sing*)	JOCKEY & KATHLEEN (*Sing*)	RONNIE (*Sings*)
Tired of		
Being sick		
And tired.	Bored	Bored.
I'm so bored		
	Sick!	
		I'm sick
Sick!		And tired
		I'm tired of
		Bein'
Tired!	Tired!	Tired of bein'
		Sick,
		Tired of bein'
Bored!	Bored!	Sick and tired,
		Tired of bein'
	My	Sick and tired.
	Ass is bored	
	Off.	
That's the problem		My ass is bored off.
	The main problem	
Love!	Is—	No stimulation!
No stimulation,	No stimulation	No stimulation!
No stimulation,	No stimulation,	
No stimulation.	Never mind	Never mind.
	Satisfaction	Satisfaction.
	I'll take	I'll take satisfaction
Is there a mind	Stimulation.	
Left to rot?		Satisfaction.
Stimulate,	You don't need	Stimulate,
Stimulate	No mind if you got	Stimulate,
	Soul.	Oh oh, Stroke my soul.
Stimulate the		
Soul inmate.		
	Stimulate,	Fight with me baby.
I'll go to the hole.	Stimulate.	
	I'll go with you.	
But		
Then they'll put us		

EL TORO, CHAMP
& OX TAIL (*Sing*)
In separate holes.
I'm
Ready, I'm
Ready, oh yes,
I'm ready!
Stimulate this
Little old inmate.
Flash me a scratch,
Flash me a be-bop
On the side of
My head
Flash me a punch
Flash me a snatch.

I need it!
Anything!
One more time to
Walk with a flash
On my patch,
One more time to
Roll out to freedom
One more time to
Walk in Jerusalem
One more time,
One more time to
Feel the—

And the sun on my arms
One more time,
One more time,

JOCKEY &
KATHLEEN (*Sing*)
But
Think of the fun
We'll have getting
There.
Oh please let
Me out of here!

RONNIE (*Sings*)
But
Think of the fun
We'll have getting
There.
Stimulate this
Little old inmate.
Flash me a scratch,
Flash me a be-bop
On the side of
My head.
Flash me a punch.
Flash me a snatch.
Flash!

Flash! Flash!
One more time to
Walk with a flash
On my patch
One more time to
Roll out to freedom
One more time to
Feel the flash of cash,
One more time,
One more time to
Feel the
Cold on my nose.

One more time,
One more time.

Oh, I'm ready!
Oh, I'm ready
to be
An eternal incar-
cerate.
Just one more
Time, get me
flashing,–

EL TORO, CHAMP
&OX TAIL (*Sing*)

JOCKEY &
KATHLEEN (*Sing*)
Just one more time
Make me happy to be
Walking,
Be happy to be walking,
Be happy to be walking.
Flash!
I got the
Fascination
With stimulation.
Flash me a scratch.
I got the fascination
With the stimulation.
Flash me a patch.
I got the
Fascination with the
Stimulation,
Fascination with the
Stimulation.
One more time.
One more time.

RONNIE (*Sings*)

Flash me a scratch,
Flash me a be-bop
On the side
Of my head,
Flash me a punch,
Flash me a snatch.

Oh, I'm ready,
Oh, I'm ready

Flash me a scratch,
Flash me a be-bop
On the side
Of my head,
Flash me a punch,
Flash me a snatch,
Flash!

I need it!
Anything!
One more time
To walk with a
Flash on my patch.
One more time to

To be
An eternal
Incarcer-
ate.

Just one more
Time to get me flashing,
Just one more time

Flash! Flash!
One more time,
Walk with a
Flash on my patch.
One more time to

Roll out to freedom
One more time to
Walk in Jerusalem.

Make me happy to be
walking.
Be happy to be walking,
Be happy to be walking.
Flash, I got the

Roll out to freedom.
One more time to
Feel the flash of cash

EL TORO, CHAMP &OX TAIL (*Sing*)	JOCKEY & KATHLEEN (*Sing*)	RONNIE (*Sings*)
One more time,	Fascination with the Stimulation.	One more time,
One more time To feel the—	Flash me a scratch	One more time To feel the
	I got the	Cold on my nose
And the sun on	Fascination with	
My arms.	The stimulation.	
One more time	Flash me a patch.	One more time,
To walk in	I got the	Walk in
Jerusalem,	Fascination with the Stimulation.	Jerusalem,
Holding hands	Fascination	Holding hands
With my love	With the stimulation.	With my love.
One more time.	One more time,	One more time,
One more time.	One more time.	One more time.

All hold. RONNIE *turns to the* OTHERS, *who feel good having played out their fantasies. They sit around. The following scene is a continuation of the scene before the song.*

RONNIE: Look inside. It isn't boring in there. (*Taps her head*) Nehru wrote twenty-six books in jail. Elizabeth Gurley Flynn wrote a damn good one, too.

EL TORO: Ney—who?

JOCKEY: Are you writing?

RONNIE: Takes too much time away from listening.

JOCKEY: Come again?

RONNIE: (*Grabs* JOCKEY *intimately and slightly rough*) I'd be happy to teach you, if you truly want to learn. I'm a Leo and have dominion over children. I haven't time for kidding or mockery. I'm interested in beauty. (*Looks around, chooses* CYNTHIA, *mainly as a lesson for* JOCKEY) I need clear eyes to look into, and beautiful skin to keep me giving. (*To* JOCKEY) If you change your dietary habits to improve your looks, I'll consider sharing some discoveries with you. (*Slaps* JOCKEY *playfully but firmly)* If you want to know—really "know"—demonstrate this to me by getting hold of yourself and improving your health habits. (*To* KATHLEEN)

RONNIE: And you, there, you're too short. Hold your torso up, get your head out of your neck. (*Turns and walks toward the cells*)

CHAMP: Christ, she's a Leo, all right.

EL TORO: I'm sorry I talked to her.

KATHLEEN: Do you think she did it?

EL TORO: Who cares?

JOCKEY: (*Dreamily looking after her*) I'm in love.

Others laugh, call her a masochist, etc.

At O.M.T. the following scene was played with physical action juxtaposed to the lines: before saying a line, the actor selects a physical contact activity and imposes it on another. The one "imposed on" has to decide to go along with it or resist. The one "imposing her will" continues the activity until replaced by a stronger will. The action imposed should have no logical connection with the line said. A different will (intention) is imposed with each line.

KATHLEEN *and* CHAMP *come up behind* JOCKEY, *bring her to the middle of the prison yard.*

KATHLEEN: What are they putting in our food?

CHAMP: What food?

JOCKEY: That ain't no food, man—where I come from the roaches turn their noses up at it.

KATHLEEN: I'm so tired all the time.

JOCKEY: They mean for us to be.

CHAMP: That's right—they mean for us to be, so's we can't be mean.

JOCKEY: And our pee turns green.

CHAMP: Only thing to do is to quit.

KATHLEEN: I've quit. I can't hold out. I don't want to get out of bed.

CHAMP: You got to quit eating the food.

JOCKEY: They got it all drugged up.

CHAMP: They throwed us in here for drugs, and they's using more on us than the Mafia ever brought across the border.

JOCKEY: You notice Witch-Freak don't talk no more.

CHAMP: I noticed.

KATHLEEN: What'd they do to her?

JOCKEY: They hit her with eight Thorazine. Everytime she looks like she's gonna say somethin', they give her another.

KATHLEEN: I had a Thorazine once, and I didn't wake up for 36 hours.

CHAMP: We all got different chemistry. You's a cheap date, baby. (*All laugh*)

KATHLEEN: I don't have the strength to write a letter.

CHAMP: You got a lover on the streets?

KATHLEEN: Yeah, yeah. I know where she is, too.

CHAMP: Do she know where you is?

JOCKEY *and* CHAMP *look at each other. A slight nod passes between them.*

JOCKEY: She on your list to get mail?

KATHLEEN: I wouldn't do that. I don't want them to know about her.

CHAMP: Where'd you meet? I love love stories.

KATHLEEN: Church picnic.

CHAMP & JOCKEY: (*Laughing*) Oh yeah? Oh yeah? O wow! What a scene!

KATHLEEN: Well it was. She was from another state. She had

a special way of talking. It sounded like singing—but I know she was talking straight to me.

JOCKEY: You got religion?

KATHLEEN: She's my God now—I know no other. It was in the middle of the song I was singing. She was standing beside me, I felt her looking at me, and my voice grew stronger. Then I thought I was getting taller—I looked down at my feet, but I got dizzy. All the people in the audience were looking up at me and they smiled. I turned my head just a bit in the middle of a note, and I caught this blaze in her eyes and I got even stronger. My voice went out to the trees. I handed her the mike. I didn't need it to reach the people. She turned off the mike and held my hand. I sang for an hour, then she helped me from the stage. We went straight to my tent.

JOCKEY: Did you make love?

KATHLEEN: We didn't have too. She was still holding my hand. The light in her eyes nearly blinded me. They were the clearest, lightest blue I've ever seen. Whenever I looked directly at her the heavens opened up behind her head, and rays came from her body—rays that held me up, rays that drew me to her. She didn't know she had these rays.. They were invisible. I could feel them as sure as I can feel this floor. I knew I could never fall again. Knew I would never fall. All I would have to do is think about her eyes, and they would always see me—and see her body and she would always hold me.

CHAMP: And that's all you did?

JOCKEY: You didn't make out?

KATHLEEN: Leave me alone. I can't get it together.

JOCKEY: You should get more protein, girl.

KATHLEEN: I thought you said we should quit eating.

JOCKEY: Well, we should probably try it and get our systems cleaned out. But I personally don't think you're strong enough.

They freeze in the last "will imposed" and begin a section of "walks."
JOCKEY *crosses to* OX TAIL'S *cell, where twinkle lights blink on.*

OX TAIL: I made a big mistake.

JOCKEY: *(Joins her in cell)* I thought you were gonna play the field from now on.

OX TAIL: I'm stuck.

CHAMP: Do you realize how many times you've been in love in the last two years?

OX TAIL: The more it happens, the harder it hits. I thought you got used to stuff like this.

RONNIE: *(Struts through prison yard to* OX TAIL'S *cell)* the cool like me, we never fall. We let them fall for *us.* Now me, I got two women working for my validation. Women got to be trained. Can't let them get the upper hand. Even the screws know that. They get out of line, you kick their ass—they'll get down on their knees and kiss your foot. I'm fixing to add another wife soon. You watch how I break the new one in. You do what I do, and you won't feel low down and blue no more. You understand?

(Sings) Look around you, hon.
Everywhere y' see—
In the prison yard
Or mincing on TV.

You see nothin', hon.
You see nothin', hon.
But a bunch of
Beautiful babes.
Everyone—guarded
By guns.

ALL: *(Sing softly under)*
Hi ya, Betty
Hello Nancy.

Come out Barbara.
Come back Marilyn.
I love Lucy,

Ethel too.
Why don't *you*
Run for
President—Rose?

ALL: We're all Babes in the Bighouse,
We're all Babes in the Bighouse,
We're all Babes in the Bighouse,
Trained to love the son of a gun!

RONNIE: So-o-o-o-o-o-o's—the
Only the way to go
Is to let nothin' show.   (*Others softly repeat "Hello Betty" etc.*)
You gotta be cool
If you wanna do
Easy time like me.

ALL: We're all Babes in the Bighouse,
We're all Babes in the Bighouse,
We're all Babes in the Bighouse,
Trained to love the son of a gun!

RONNIE: These women are confused,
Broken and abused,
So how do I show my class—?
I kick 'em in the ass!

ALL: We're all Babes in the Bighouse,
We're all Babes in the Bighouse,
We're all Babes in the Bighouse,
Trained to love the son of a gun!

RONNIE: Follow my simple golden rule.
Show 'em who's boss—
Nobody fools the cool—
Nail her to the cross!

ALL: Babes in the Bighouse,
Babes in the Bighouse,
The bughouse,
The Bighouse—
Hello Babes!
Hello Babes!

(Up you, Mister!
Free my sister!)
We're all Babes in the Bighouse,
Babes! Babes! Babes!

*Lights come up suddenly on the warden's area, in front of the net.
EL TORO has transformed into GLORIA SWENSON and is being
interrogated by MATRONS 1 and 2 (JOCKEY and CHAMP). All three
face the audience with the MATRONS standing directly behind
GLORIA.*

MATRON 1: At O-six hundred hours, Gloria Swenson, you
were reported by Officer McClannahan on June 12 (*You may
substitute a date closer to performance date*) to be seen in a passion-
ate embrace in the shower with Mary Lou Wiseman. We have
rules here, Gloria. This is a very serious offense. Do you have
anything to say?

GLORIA: I need another shower.

MATRON 2: Insolence is also against the rules.

MATRON 1: Do you wish to compound the charge against you?

GLORIA: I really do need a shower. I haven't been allowed a
shower in more than a week.

MATRON 2: Why not?

GLORIA: Officer McClannahan took my shower privileges
away for talking too loud at dinner.

MATRON 1: You were identified by Officer McClannahan to
be in the shower with Mary Lou Wiesman. Is that true?

GLORIA: To quote our beloved ex-President, "I can't recall."

MATRON 2: (*Snaps GLORIA'S head around to look her in the eyes*)
President who?

MATRON 1: (*Gives MATRON 2 a signal to release GLORIA, then
smiles and continues in her own style*) Are you a member of that
secret cult?

GLORIA: Yes.

MATRON 1: (*As if she's forgotten*) What's the name of it?

GLORIA: (*Sotto voce*) Jeffersonian Democracy.

MATRON 2: *(Excited—snaps* GLORIA'S *head around again)* What?

GLORIA: Jefferson— . . .

MATRON 1 *more aggressively signals* MATRON 2 *to leave the interrogation to her.*

MATRON 1: (*Sizing up* GLORIA'S *"insolence" she holds her around the shoulders*) Loooooooooook, Gloria, we're here to help you. Are you going to cooperate and give your side of the story? Or do we accept Officer McClannahan's report and punish you accordingly?

GLORIA: Officer McClannahan lied.

MATRON 1: Why would Officer McClannahan lie?

GLORIA: (*Animated*) I don't know. But I do need a shower. Here—(*lifts her arms*) smell me.

MATRONS *move to the right.* MATRON 1 *kneels,* MATRON 2 *places her chin on* MATRON 1'S *head. They drop their jaws, mouths hanging "dumb" in a "helplessness" image, then take the line from this position.*

MATRONS: That is not ladylike behavior. (*They repeat the image*)

GLORIA: Ladies take showers twice a day. You only let me have a shower once a week. I can't stand my own smell.

MATRON 1: (*Moving back to her position behind* GLORIA) When did you stop engaging in homosexual behavior with Mary Lou Wiseman?

GLORIA: When I stopped beating my husband.

MATRON 2: (*Pauses—turns* GLORIA'S *head, looks into her eyes*) Look, Gloria, we do not appreciate these smart remarks. It's going to have to be entered on your record. Is this the sort of record you want to go before your parole board?

GLORIA: No ma'am.

MATRON 1 *gives* MATRON 2 *a sign that she'll handle it now.*

MATRON 1: (*Embracing* GLORIA, *who looks at arms around her and laughs to herself*) All right, we're getting somewhere. Now, we want to help you straighten yourself out and get along here. You want to have a clean record, don't you?

GLORIA: I want to have a clean record and I want to have a clean body.

MATRONS *move to left, repeat "helpless" image in a slightly different combination with* MATRON 2 *squatting,* MATRON 1 *on top. They drop their jaws.*

MATRONS: Put her in Adjustment until she decides to answer our questions like a rational human being. (*They repeat image, mouths hanging open and maintain this through next speech*)

GLORIA: I ain't done anything. You can't put me in the hole for smelling bad. It's your fault. You don't even give hot water. I want some soap. Soap? I haven't been near a shower in more than two weeks. You liars. You ladies. You lady liars. Come out of your closets, you bulldykes, you secret cunt cocksuckers! You're the liars! You're the liars!

MATRON 2: Take her away.

MATRON 2 *removes her guard coat and becomes* JOCKEY *again.* GLORIA/EL TORO *puts on guard coat and transforms into a* MATRON. RONNIE, *as a* MATRON 1, *watches the audience as she crosses the space, takes a place in the platform in front of the net.* EL TORO, RONNIE *and* CHAMP *impose their wills on one another physically or watch prisoners and audience for trouble as they sing.* JOCKEY, KATHLEEN, OX TAIL *and* CYNTHIA, *in their cells, work on "finding a way out"—they move and step together as they sing.*

MATRONS: (*Sing*) This is occupied territory.

PRISONERS: (*Sing*) We live in occupied territory.
Are you ready to love
Beyond your fingernail?
There is a vast body to behold—
That body is you.

MATRONS: (*Reaching out to* PRISONERS)
I implore you to swim into the
Mainstream of your own conscious being,
And live in your whole body, too.

Aren't you cramped there, under that
Damp, dirty nail?

PRISONERS: (*To audience*) (*Describing prison life*)
Expand outward into your fist.
Let your mind exist in
Your chest and rise upward to
The tip of your breast.

ALL: Ahhhhhhhh yes, she feels so good—
And you can feel you, if you only would.

MATRONS *move slowly toward* PRISONERS *with outstretched arms.
The* PRISONERS *are suddenly free—this is a fantasy section. The cells
open, they crawl out.*

JOCKEY *and* KATHLEEN *run hand in hand "like youth in the wood,"
in and out of the line of* MATRONS. OX TAIL *and* CYNTHIA *sing
to each other.* MATRONS *still sing to the women.*

ALL: Let me hold your hand,
And you can live here safely in my land.
I won't give anyone your
Phone number,
But you can call me any time—
Night or day—
And we will—

PRISONERS *embrace,* MATRONS *try to pull them apart—more "imposing of will."*

ALL: Fling our arms around each other—

Tug-of war between embracing PRISONERS *and* MATRONS *trying to
separate them continues.*

ALL: And lay and lay land lay
And lay and lay
And lay.

CHAMP *transforms from* MATRON *back to herself and begins scrubbing.* RONNIE (*as* MATRON) *pulls* KATHLEEN *from* JOCKEY'S *arms
and throws her to the floor.* KATHLEEN *immediately starts scrubbing
toward* CHAMP. RONNIE *and* EL TORO *transform back to prisoners.*
PRISONERS *"walk" the yards and corridors as* KATHLEEN *and* CHAMP
scrub.

CHAMP: I had a very high standard of living at the Federal Facility. Worked in the laundry and had forty customers a month.

KATHLEEN: How much?

CHAMP: That's a carton of cigarettes per customer.

KATHLEEN: You were rich.

CHAMP: It was real easy time. Some of the women there wanted to look sharp all the time. Know what I mean? And I got paid in cash to starch clothes for the officers.

KATHLEEN: Could you keep it?

RONNIE *is feeling full of herself—she looks around for a conquest, selects* EL TORO, *approaches her and roughly sends her to the cells to get ready, "walks" and watches to make sure that no one saw her speak to* EL TORO.

CHAMP: Naw, it added to my account in the Commissary. But I had anything I wanted there. Anything! I never been so poor in my life as I am here.

KATHLEEN: Me too. There isn't a big enough population to build up a really good bank account.

CHAMP: (*Agreeing*) Tell me about it.

They continue to scrub. RONNIE *taps* CHAMP *on the back— a signal that* CHAMP *should be lookout while* RONNIE *"tends to some business."* CHAMP *gleefully runs off to do this.* EL TORO *waits anxiously in* RONNIE'S *cell—finally* RONNIE *cooly joins her.*

RONNIE: (*Not even looking at* TORO *—looking out bars*) Lay down on your stomach.

EL TORO: (*Touching* RONNIE) Look, I really like you.

RONNIE: (*Shakes her off*) Hurry—we don't have any time.

EL TORO: I love the way your nose goes. You got the same perfect nose as Farrah Fawcett.

RONNIE: (*Forces her down*) No shit! Lay down on this mat.

EL TORO: (*Reaches for her*) I really dig you.

RONNIE: (*Twists her arm*) Then do like I say.

EL TORO: But I want to get to know you. (*Tries to kiss her*)

RONNIE: (*Moves away*) I don't go for mush.

EL TORO: (*Hanging on* RONNIE) It's only a little kiss—what you in for?

RONNIE: (*Forces* EL TORO *flat onto mat*) For a while.

EL TORO: You're strong.

RONNIE: (*Over* TORO) That's right. Turn over.

EL TORO: But I want to look at you. Your face knocks me out.

RONNIE: Take a good look (*Poses*) and turn over.

EL TORO *tries to kiss her some more*—RONNIE *twists her arm til she turns over onto her stomach.*

EL TORO: Hey, at least let me take off my clothes.

RONNIE: (*Leaps onto her*) No time.

EL TORO: Oh, please baby, let's undress if we're gonna make love. I'm crazy about you, baby—you send me around the band. Please. Let's take our clothes off.

RONNIE: (*Putting all her weight on* EL TORO *and beginning to gyrate*) Don't talk. This is the way I do it! I want you to say, "Daddy, my ass is yours."

EL TORO *goes into gales of laugher.* RONNIE *gets off, furious, and shakes her.*

RONNIE: Say it!

EL TORO: (*Laughing some more*) You're a riot?

RONNIE: (*Twisting* EL TORO'S *arm higher, pulling her up so both are kneeling*) I told you not to frustrate your Daddy, little Mama, or I'll have to whip you.

EL TORO: You can't be serious. Hey, I dig you, but this isn't any fun.

RONNIE: (*Pushes her down*) If you dig me, (*Crushes her with her weight*) then you'll please me.

EL TORO: (*Cries out*) You're heavy!

RONNIE: (*Begins to gyrate, pumping on* EL TORO'S *behind*) O Mama, O Mama. You got a beautiful ass. It's all for me, ain't it, Mama? Give me your ass, Little Mama—give your Daddy your great big beautiful ass. Give it to me. (*Pause*) Say it! (*Pause*) Say it! Say, "Daddy, my ass is yours." (*Pause*) Say it!

EL TORO: You're hurting me.

RONNIE: Say it, Mama—tell me. Tell me what you'll give me. Tell me.

EL TORO: Please, let me go. You're crushing me.

RONNIE: (*Bearing down harder, approaching climax*) Say it!

EL TORO: (*Very flat—to get it over with*) Daddy . . . my . . . ass . . . is . . . yours . . .

RONNIE: (*Reaching climax in sighs and spasms, she cries out*) Oh, Mama . . . (*Whoops, and climbs the bars as high as she can climb*) I love you!

Lights come up abruptly on the net area. TERESA (KATHLEEN) *is "strapped" into the chair, the* DOCTOR (JOCKEY) *talking to her. This action began taking place during previous scene in mime on* RONNIE'S *line: "no time,"* JOCKEY *puts on white lab coat and transforms into* DOCTOR, *choses* CYNTHIA *to help her set up examining room. They cross to the warden's area in front of the net and prepare for a psychiatric examination, setting a large silver arm chair with straps on the platform. (In the O.M.T. production, a male mannikin dressed as a "pimp" was set behind the chair, his arms placed on the patients' shoulders instead of straps)* KATHLEEN *has transformed into* TERESA—DOCTOR (JOCKEY) *directs* CYNTHIA *to bring* TERESA *into the examining room and after she does, dismisses her back to her cell.*

DOCTOR: *You* know why you're here, don't you Teresa? Don't you?

TERESA: I didn't start it.

DOCTOR: But you finished it, didn't you, Teresa? Juanita has a broken jaw, and a broken collar bone. She's the fifth woman you've put in the hospital. You fight too much, Teresa. Women should not fight. It isn't ladylike, is it? You lose your femininity when you fight like a man. Don't you, Teresa?

TERESA: (*Under her breath, but audible*) I could knock you on your ass, too.

DOCTOR: No you can't. You're strapped to the table.

TERESA: I promise I won't fight no more.

DOCTOR: You promised that last time.

TERESA: But I promise. It wasn't my fault. I had to protect myself. Juanita started it.

DOCTOR: Did Caroline start it? (*Mock-throws a kiss into the air*) Did Dawn start it? (*Mock throws another kiss*)

TERESA: I'll be perfect. I won't talk to anyone. You can put me in Adjustment, but please don't give me that shot.

DOCTOR: Oh—(*Pulls out an oversize hypodermic needle*) you remember.

TERESA: (*Trying to pull away*) I'm sorry. I'm really sorry. If I had it to do over again, I'd just hold on to that little shit Juanita until the matron came. I would. I promise I would. I didn't mean to hurt her—she's just jealous. She fell. She did this to get me here.

DOCTOR: You did this, Teresa. (*Flips* TERESA *around so the side of her bottom is exposed, rubs it with alcohol*) This should remind you not to fight. (DOCTOR *backs up, takes aim with hypo and with a big sweeping movement, lands on target*)

TERESA: (*Crys and pleads*) Please don't give it to me. It makes me feel like I'm dying. Please don't . . . please . . .

TERESA *begins to shake all over and gasp for breath—this continues throughout* DOCTOR'S *speech. The injection is a muscle relaxant—the lung muscles are among those affected, so that involuntary (natural) breathing is made impossible, giving patient the feeling of drowning or suffocating.*

DOCTOR: (*Removing the needle*) You have to learn to act like a lady, Teresa. You can't throw your fists into the face of anyone who does something you don't like. We can't have a world like that, Teresa. Every time you fight, you're going to get one of these.

DOCTOR: (*Holds up hypo, though* TERESA *by this time is gasping for air*) You must calm yourself, and decide you are going to be a lady (*Moves behind net*) and be good and kind to your fellow inmates and to all the people here who have your best interests at heart. You know, Teresa, we have only your best interests at heart. You have to become a lady so that we can help you.

OX TAIL, CHAMP, CYNTHIA *and* EL TORO *wheel a tray of cosmetics toward* TERESA—*they can work with stewardess images. As* DOCTOR *continues her lecture,* PRISONERS *apply eye makeup, rouge, lipstick, spray deodorant, nail polish and perfume to* TERESA'S *body.* TERESA *continues to suffer convulsions and gasp for air*—PRISONERS *help restrain her when the gasping and convulsions get too great. Audience must be allowed to see that the other* PRISONERS *really care for* TERESA, *but that they must follow orders or they might be in her place next.*

DOCTOR: You have to keep your dress on and stop walking like a cowboy. You have to start wearing the nice lipstick we allow you. You can make enough money working here to buy the nice lipstick and mascara, and hairspray and perfume you're allowed to wear now. [*Note: After orientation* PRISONERS *are given some makeup privileges.*] You know, in the old days, ladies here weren't even permitted to get dressed up and pretty. But now you can go to the beauty parlor and learn to fix your hair real nice in all the latest man-catching styles. You can get yourself real fixed up here, Teresa. So when you get out, if you shape up, you can get yourself a husband and settle down and live like a normal human being. And raise a family and cook and care for your man and all your little children and be kind to the people who want to help you. You want to do that, don't you, Teresa?

TERESA: (*Through gasps and cries, shaking and flailing,—the other* PRISONERS *hold her down*) Holy Mary, Mother of God . . . I'm dying. O Mother Mary, Blessed art thou. O Mother Mary, save me, save me (*Gasp for air*) Hail Mary full of grace. (*Gasp*)

Mother, I can't breath—I'm sick and drowning—take me in your arms. I adore you, Holy Mother.

DOCTOR: (*Calmly in control*) If you promise you'll never fight again and will obey all the rules, and understand we are only here to help you and see you develop in your best interests, (*Spreads arms, opens them to heaven in "Christ's ascension" image*) I-will-save-your-life.

TERESA: Mary will save my life!

DOCTOR: (*Maintaining image*) Mary and *I* will save your life!

TERESA: Only the Mother of God can do that. (*Gasping and convulsions—goes into fit*)

DOCTOR: (*Leaps out from behind net, slowly approaches* TERESA) You act like the worst kind of criminal male, Teresa! There is a long list of complaints against you! (*Builds and builds till she loses control*) You cut another woman's face with a home-made knife! You stole baby pictures from Johanna! You beat Juanita till she had to go to the hospital! (*Calming herself, regaining control*) If you don't pull yourself together and start to act like a feminine person, you'll get more of these injections.

TERESA: (*Goes into convulsions—other* PRISONERS *restrain her*) I can't stand it. I'm dying. Hail Mary full of grace.

DOCTOR: Do you promise never to fight again, Teresa? (TERESA *retches and gasps, the* OTHERS *hold her*) Do you promise to act like a lady? (*Slowly* TERESA *and other* PRISONERS *nod in unison*) I can't hear you, Teresa. Answer me like a lady.

They continue nodding. Others get up and walk like zombies nodding toward their cells. TERESA *remains in chair, nodding.*

DOCTOR: Do you promise you will become a feminine person, demure and self-controlled? To smile whenever you see me walk by? To control your temper and learn to walk like a sexy woman? Do you promise, Teresa? (TERESA *nods*) I can't hear you. Ladies know how to speak.

TERESA: (*Nodding*) I . . . pro —mise . . .

DOCTOR *smiles and injects sedative. Lights dim and come up on*

RONNIE'S *cell.* TERESA *crawls to cells on her stomach.*

RONNIE: (*Shouts to the whole prison yard, especially at* OX TAIL, EL TORO, CYNTHIA *and* CHAMP *who are nodding and walking like zombies*) Awwww, you commie prudes give me a pain where a pill can't reach. Why, if we lived in any of them commie countries, we'd be shot or put in jail.

CHAMP *and others re-enter the present and cross to their cells, no longer zombie-like.*

CHAMP: *Hell,* we are in jail.

RONNIE: I mean, we'd be in jail for being gay. Just for that, stupid—'stead of what we *are* in for. I mean, if I was clean of everything, *everything*—but just I was gay—they'd shoot me or put me in an insane asylum if I wouldn't go straight.

CHAMP: You'd get proper help.

RONNIE: Goddamn it, that's just what I mean! *You* think *I'm* sick! Listen, you nearsighted Marxist. I *chose* to be gay. I chose a woman to defy the man. It was a political act (*Raises fist*) and (*Rubs herself on bars*) it was a sex act. (*Busts herself up laughing*) Trouble with you guys is, you got zippers on yer pussies, there's padlocks on the zippers, and you have forgot the combination!

CHAMP: You didn't make a political choice—you're just a pitiful victim of a repetition compulsion—

RONNIE: Thank you, Doctor. It's all in my head, so get out of bed! (*A little jivey dance*) It's all in my head so get out of bed! It's all in my head so get out of—

OX TAIL *enters, transformed into* MATRON, *faces cells from center of yard area.*

MATRON: Bedtime. (*Plays "bell sound" violin chord—*PRISONERS *come forward in their cells for the count*)

JOCKEY: Six.

CHAMP: Twelve.

KATHLEEN: Sixteen.

CYNTHIA: Twenty-nine.

EL TORO: Thirty-one.

RONNIE: Forty.

MATRON: Lock in! (*Rattles chain on cells to signify lock-up*) Lights out! (*Black out*)

CYNTHIA *puts on guard coat and transforms into the* WARDEN. *She suspends herself over to one set of scaffold cells to give the god-like quality of looking down on the prisoners. Her voice becomes a tinny drone—by denasalizing the voice she sounds like a loudspeaker. She does not hear the women—nor is she aware of the activity (the passing of contraband) going on inside the cells. The* PRISONERS *hear the* WARDEN'S *voice and go about their covert activities, cautiously passing cigarettes, dirty magazines, a vibrator, valium, etc.*

The next scene, ("Harriet the Snitch") begins as soon as the WARDEN *speaks. Both scenes play simultaneously and can be heard clearly, Visually, the main focus is on the active passing of contraband.*

WARDEN: Welcome to the Women's State Correctional Facility. There are rules to be followed here. I will give you the daily routine, rules and general procedures of our institution.

5:00 a.m. Awake culinary workers
5:30 a.m. You will be counted
6:00 a.m. Awake entire population to prepare for breakfast
7:00 a.m. Breakfast
7:30 a.m. All inmates report to place of work assignment
8:00 a.m. You will be counted
11:30 a.m. Dinner
12 noon   You will be counted
12:30 p.m. All inmates return to place of work assignment
3:00 p.m. Prepare to return to living spaces
3:30 p.m. You will be counted
4:30 p.m. Supper
5:30 p.m. You will be counted
6:30 p.m. Recreation: TV, cards and outside recreation, weather permitting
7:30 p.m. You will be counted
10:00 p.m. Lights out
10:30 p.m. You will be counted

Simultaneously with the above speech, twinkle lights come up on cells where the women are cautiously passing contraband.

CHAMP: (*Handing a small packet to* CYNTHIA) Here's your Thorazine and Librium. That's a pack.

CYNTHIA: (*Passes a pack of cigarettes to* CHAMP *in payment*) One pack. Thanks.

KATHLEEN: Stash it all—here comes the snitch!!

JOCKEY *transformed into* HARRIET, *the prison snitch—enters her cell smiling and waving to the others.*

CHAMP: (*To the others*) Watch her. She'll make you think she wants you for her old man, and then go rat on you to the screw.

The women become very busy and ignore HARRIET.

HARRIET: (*Trying to wiggle her way into the conversation*) Oh Juanita, you have the most beautiful hair. Teresa, hasn't Juanita the most beautiful hair you ever saw?

OX TAIL: Some have and some haven't.

HARRIET: Who's got a coffin nail? (*Silence*) I'm dying for a smoke. That movie they had tonight is the squarest they've had since I been in.

CHAMP: You mean you can tell the difference?

HARRIET: Hey, Dana, baby—I just love to say your real name, Dana—hey Dana baby, don't get on me, I love you. I been digging you ever since you arrived—I think you're neat. I really get off on our attitude—I'd give anything to be like you.

CHAMP: Some can and some can't.

HARRIET: I mean it, Dana. I even try to copy your walk.

CHAMP: They throw people in the hole for less than that.

HARRIET: Aww, they're not that bad, Dana. You always try to make out the staff so mean.

CHAMP: I don't do nothin—they show the world.

HARRIET: (*Laughing*) You break me up.

CHAMP: I didn't notice anything funny. (*To others*) Did you notice anything funny I said?

KATHLEEN: I didn't notice that *you* said anything funny.

HARRIET: Hey, can I have a piece of the action?

OTHER PRISONERS: (*Freezing her out*) Some can and some can't.

PRISONERS *fall into images of caged animals. The twinkle lights blink on and off as the women transform from one caged image to another. These may be a combination of still and moving images. Some images may have appeared earlier in the play. The* WARDEN *never breaks the pattern of her speech. (At O.M.T. it was always about here that the "snitch" scene was completed and the images began.)*

WARDEN: 11:45 p.m. You will be counted
2:00 a.m. You will be counted

You must keep your blouses buttoned to the top button, keep your collar out. You must eat all food you take at feeding time—all food. You will not make any comment on what goes on in our institution or about another inmate in letters sent out of our institution. You will *never* use vulgar and/or profane language. Only two people at a time may sit on a bed, and they must be sitting up with both feet on the floor. You may not speak to a visitor without permission. You will not whistle, laugh loudly or talk loud. You will always be neat and clean. You will refrain from combing your hair in the recreation room.

EL TORO: (*Comes to the front of her cell and shouts to the others*) They won't let us have nothing juicy to read!

KATHLEEN: (*Pounding on cell bars, responding to* EL TORO) Oh, what I'd give for a hot and nasty R. Crumb Comix.

CHAMP: (*At the front of her cell*) Hey, if I had a hot and dirty book to read, you think they would read it with me over the watchdog TV? Or would they come and snatch it away and read it all alone by their lonesomes in the matrons' john?

OX TAIL: (*To the others*) We could share the wealth, but they wouldn't do that, I bet— oh no!

JOCKEY, *as herself again, leaps out of her cell to the center playing area and strips down to her shorts and "coyote" t-shirt. (whether the actor strips is a directional choice.)*

JOCKEY: But hey, what if I croon a dirty book to you? They couldn't take it away, hey? No, there'd be nothing for 'em to confiscate. Nothing to go against me in my file for the parole board, because it would go right out into the air. (*Acts out the "dirty book" story as she "croons" it, transforming into a pop-art version of the aggressive male. Simultaneously the others change clothes and transform into their favorite criminals from the past*) Oh, he sighed as he stared at the juicy melons straining in their titty-tight circular-stitched Egyptian cotton bra. Oh, he cried inside his head. Oh, I want to get my hot and pulsating hands inside her shocking pink low-cut cleavage, and free those two giant cantaloupes from their cloth cages. Yes, he husked into her perfectly carved alabaster ear. Yes, my dewy angel. Yes, I love you with all my heart and soul. He felt his member swelling, compelling him toward his goal. He crushed her shocking-pink-sheathed, hot and heaving body, and ran his long, hair-matted hands down to the bottom of her bottom. And his tongue reared up in his mouth as he gazed upon the outline of her twin love buttons, pushing forward, begging to escape into his loving lips. But first he nibbled softly at the base of her neck. Softly, softly, softly. We got all night together, angel of my life. I'm going to graze my mouth over the length and breast of you before I unsheath my own pink knife.

Lights come up on RONNIE *in her cell dressed as her dream crook. The* OTHERS *stand behind her in costumes of their fantasies—the Watergate men, Al Capone, Bonnie, etc. During* RONNIE'S *next speech, the* OTHERS *transform into specific contemporary criminals and ask, plead or demand to be pardoned.*

RONNIE: When my mother and sisters
find out what you've done to me,   OX TAIL: Pardon me!
they're gonna run all the way
from home,   KATHLEEN: Pardon me!
and tear this concentration camp   JOCKEY & EL TORO:
out by the roots   Pardon me!
and throw it, bars and all, into
the Gulf of Mexico. They won't

let you do this to me.
My mother loves me.
My sisters love me.
My mother always loved me.
And when she finds out you took
her daughter away from her,
she's gonna set fire to your
feet, she's gonna set fire to
your liver, she's gonna set
fire to your eyes, and she's
gonna laugh while you scream
for *her* mercy.
You can't do this to her daughter
(*Name calling*) You Jesus-
Freak cocksuckers! You Nazis.
You rusty I-U-D's. You beer cans.
You leaky diaphragms. You WASP
lickers, you ass-kissers of the
State! (*Pause*) Let me out
of here
before my mother finds out what
you're doing to me.
This is your last chance.
You're gonna get it, you're
really gonna get it.
My mother and my sisters
love me!

CYNTHIA: Pardon me!
OX TAIL: Pardon me.
EL TORO: Pardon me.
KATHLEEN & JOCKEY: Pardon me.
CYNTHIA: Pardon me!

OX TAIL & JOCKEY: Pardon me.

KATHLEEN: Pardon me.

EL TORO: Pardon me.
CYNTHIA: Pardon me.

OX TAIL: Pardon me.

PRISONERS *begin speak-singing "pardon me" from their cells, each on own dissonant note.*

JOCKEY: Pardon me!

EL TORO: Pardon me!

ALL: Pardon me!

RONNIE: Oh gee, pardon me.

CHAMP: Oh see Spot. Pardon me.

OX TAIL & CYNTHIA: Oh we saw him—Gerry Ford—Pardon the bastards and the thieving Spots.

JOCKEY: I got caught!

ALL: I got caught,
But I wasn't meant to—

JOCKEY: I got caught.

KATHLEEN: I got caught.

ALL: But I wasn't meant to—

EL TORO: They only caught the ones in the right spot.

CHAMP & RONNIE: And they didn't mean it.

ALL: We all know they didn't mean it.

CHAMP & RONNIE: They're very mean—

ALL: But they didn't mean that.

OX TAIL, CYNTHIA & KATHLEEN: They only had *their* best interests at heart,
And they don't want to be apart
From their wives and daughters.

JOCKEY, RONNIE & CHAMP: And they sure as fucking far-out won't change their spots!

RONNIE: They're in the right spot.

JOCKEY: Pardon me.

EL TORO: Pardon me.

OX TAIL: Pardon me.

CYNTHIA: Pardon me.

JOCKEY: I agree you caught me.

RONNIE: You caught me red-handed and I did it.

EL TORO: But it made me feel sad.

KATHLEEN: You'll feel glad—

ALL: If you'll pardon me.

CYNTHIA: Pardon me.

CHAMP: Pardon me.

RONNIE: Pardon me.

ALL: Pardon me! (*Beat*) Pardon me! (*Beat*) Par-don-ME!!!!

ALL HOLD

BLACK OUT

Special thanks to the women and men in prison in the U.S. and Canada who asked us to make this play.

This play has been the most popular in our repertoire to date. The following people appeared in BABES at various times:

Jill Anderson	Nancy Larson	Linda Griffith
Joe Guinan	Michael Malstead	Mary Thatcher
Judith Katz	JoAnn Schmidman	Stephanie Toothacher
Jim Laferla	Rae Ann Schmitz	Donna Young
James Larson	Elisa Stacy	

The music was written by John Sheehan and Jill Anderson and is available upon request.

The net was designed by Diane Degan

Lighting was designed by Judy Gillespie and Colbert McClellan

The original production of this piece was made possible in part by grants from the Rockefeller Foundation and the National Endowment For the Arts.

BATTERY

BY DANIEL THERRIAULT

Electricity is the central metaphor and an expressive image
for this unusual love story set in an electrical workshop.

DEATH in the POT

by Manuel Van Loggem

An English-style thriller with a fascinating plot that takes intricate twists and turns, as a husband and wife try to kill each other off, aided by a mysterious Merchant of Death. Mr. Van Loggem's works have been widely produced throughout Europe.

ESCOFFIER
KING OF CHEFS
by
Owen S. Rackleff

©Tom V.H.

In this one-man show set in a Monte Carlo villa at the end of the last century, the grand master of the kitchen, Escoffier, ponders a glorious return from retirement. In doing so, he relates ancedotes about the famous and shares his mouth-watering recipes with the audience.

LOOKING-GLASS

by Michael Sutton and Cynthia Mandelberg

This provocative chronicle, interspersed with fantasy sequences from ALICE IN WONDERLAND, traces the career of Charles Dodgson (better known as Lewis Carroll) from his first work on the immortal classic, to his downfall when accused of immortality.

LOSING TIME

BY JOHN HOPKINS

Jane Alexander, Shirley Knight and Tony Roberts won critical acclaim at the award-winning Manhattan Theatre Club for their work in this powerful drama about relationships traumatized by a violent sexual assault. NOTE: Play Contains Explicit Language.

A presentation of magical and possible events in the lives of two women born in the last century.

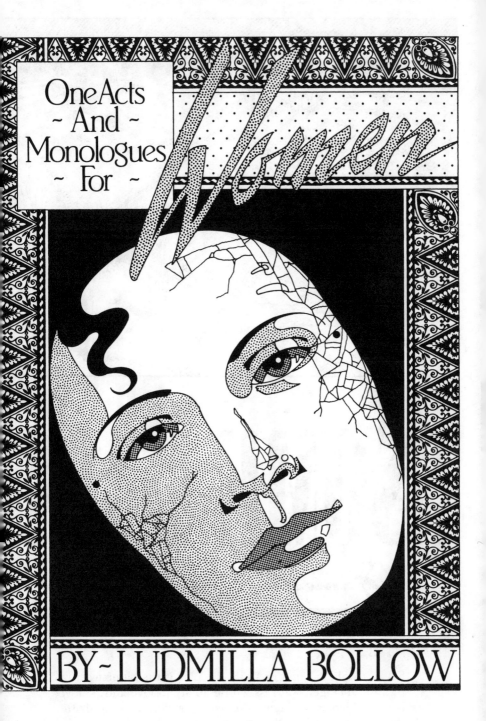

One Acts
~ And ~
Monologues
~ For ~
Women

BY ~ LUDMILLA BOLLOW

These haunting plays mark the arrival of a new voice in the American Theater.

SOME RAIN

by James Edward Luczak

Set in rural Alabama in 1968, the play is the bittersweet tale of a middle-aged waitress whose ability to love and be loved is re-kindled by her chance encounter with a young drifter. First presented in 1982 at the Eugene O'Neill Playwright's Conference and Off-Broadway on Theatre Row.

SUMMIT CONFERENCE

ROBERT DAVID MACDONALD

n the Berlin chancellery in 1941, this play is a fictional encounter between
Braun and Clara Petacci. This show had a successful run on London's West
 in 1982 with Glenda Jackson.

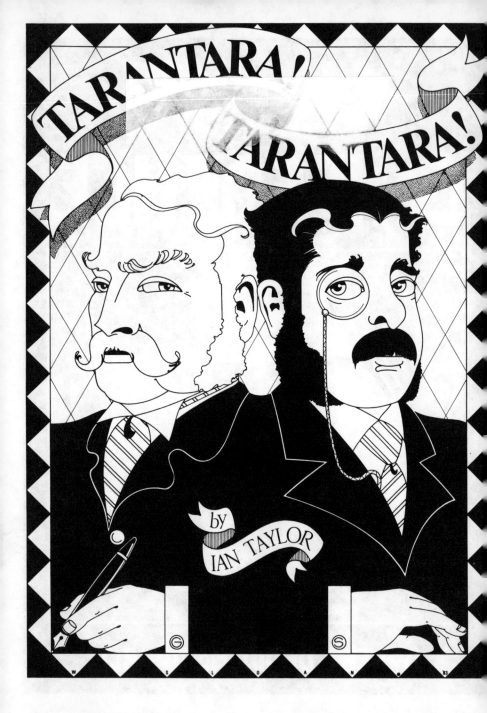

TARANTARA! TARANTARA!

by IAN TAYLOR

This delightful small-scale musical is about the life of Gilbert and Sullivan. It
intersperced with some of the best known songs from the Savy operas, includir
THE PIRATES OF PENZANCE, HMS PINAFORE and THE MIKADO. Th
show had a very successful run on the West End of London in 1975.